Unfinished
BUSINESS

*For Madalyn
my best
Nadine S.*

***Unfinished* BUSINESS**

THE MOTHER TRUCKER

Nadine Shelby Schramm

Copyright © 2015 Nadine Shelby Schramm.

All rights reserved. No part of this book may be used or reproduced by any means, graphic, electronic, or mechanical, including photocopying, recording, taping or by any information storage retrieval system without the written permission of the publisher except in the case of brief quotations embodied in critical articles and reviews.

Archway Publishing books may be ordered through booksellers or by contacting:

Archway Publishing
1663 Liberty Drive
Bloomington, IN 47403
www.archwaypublishing.com
1 (888) 242-5904

Because of the dynamic nature of the Internet, any web addresses or links contained in this book may have changed since publication and may no longer be valid. The views expressed in this work are solely those of the author and do not necessarily reflect the views of the publisher, and the publisher hereby disclaims any responsibility for them.

Any people depicted in stock imagery provided by Thinkstock are models, and such images are being used for illustrative purposes only. Certain stock imagery © Thinkstock.

ISBN: 978-1-4808-1868-2 (sc)
ISBN: 978-1-4808-1869-9 (e)

Library of Congress Control Number: 2015945554

Print information available on the last page.

Archway Publishing rev. date: 7/27/2015

To Bud Schramm, who did so much for me by
giving me a life I did not know even existed.
I dedicate this to him for his love.

Then to all my family and the people
who have helped me in my troubled times
and who shared all my great times.

Contents

Introduction	ix
My Childhood; A Farmer's Daughter	1
My World Turned Upside Down	21
Ups And Downs of Getting my Life Back Together	33
The Same Old Fear	41
Changes to a Better Life	51
A Very Complicated Time	75
To the Good Times	99
My Prayers Answered	119
New Endeavors and Intrigue	141
One Happy Grandma	169
The Last Trip with Bud, but the Best	189
Success, with Help from Many Great People	209
Politics, Business, and Fun	227
Special times with Family	267
Earning Honors, and Making New Friends along the Way	283
The Work Ethic I Learned as a Farm Girl Pays off in the Big Apple	307
One Happy Family	327

Introduction

When I evaluate my life, I realize how instrumental my childhood was in all things I did or accomplished.

My parents, Gussie Lee Brown and Hobart McKinley (Kin) Shelby, had a very difficult decision to make when they married.

My father had a hereditary ailment called retinitis pigmentosa, as did his mother. They knew he would lose his eyesight gradually and that by the age of forty or so, it would be almost gone.

Half my siblings and several nieces and nephews also carry the genes of blindness.

They chose farming even though my father had grown up as a son of a minister. My mother was from a farm family, so she knew a lot about farming. It was a good choice, and there were few in those days.

So I will tell you of a wonderful childhood being one of eleven children.

I was born just as the Great Depression of the 1930s began.

I was the sixth child, and even though they had eleven, my parents somehow made each of us feel special.

Because they were good farmers, we never went to bed hungry as so many others did. Many years later, I had a friend who told me she begged her mother to let her come stay many nights with us because she knew we had food.

We were a very big, happy family with no fighting, and we never heard our parents argue. We still all just have fun together though all the generations.

Then I endured an abusive life for several years because of a man who would now be called a stalker. I escaped with many scars.

I moved on and started four companies. I took over Budd Enterprises in 1990 when my husband Louis C. Schramm (a.k.a. Bud) died suddenly of a massive heart attack.

When I married Bud Schramm, he gave me a beautiful life I could not even imagine. He was a man who was kind, loving, and understanding.

I lost him much too young at sixty-four years of age, but I always say I have an angel on my shoulder.

I hope you enjoy this book as much as I am enjoying the journey of my life.

There was an event that has really given me different outlook on my life.

Dr. Sal Cumella invited me to lunch. As we had lunch,

he asked if he could recommend me to be an honoree for an organization by the name of New York Women's Agenda.

I did not know him personally at that time, but I had seen him at a few charity events. I was not completely sure why he wanted to recommend me. I guess he researched my background and felt that it fit the profile of past honorees since I had started four successful companies. I know many organizations, but I had never heard of this particular one.

When I heard of their past honorees, I wasn't sure if I would even qualify. However, I have never thought I could not do anything I wished. Never to use the word *can't*. So I agreed that he could put my name in.

I got a call asking to meet, and knew I was in trouble. They had vetted me. I guess I did not realize that women who are not afraid to believe in themselves were who they were looking for. That is truly me. I have always known there are no limits in being a female.

I sometimes have trouble when people talk about child labor. We all worked by the age of six picking cotton, beans, potatoes, and fruit, plus all the other things we grew.

It would be considered child abuse by today's standards, but it was normal in our day, and I had no problem with all of us working—and my brothers and sisters didn't, either. We sure did not get into trouble as so many do today because they have too much time on their hands. You will see that I reveled in doing my share.

That was an age most of the young leaders of today would not recognize. We needed to work at a very young age to eat and contribute to our family's ability to survive.

I was picked by New York Women's Agenda. I needed to avoid embarrassing my nominator.

What do I need to do on the big day? I realized I just needed to give thanks for being awarded the designation and share my life journey.

I love to talk and can for hours with friends and am never at a loss for words. And I'm perfectly comfortable speaking to small groups, but speaking to this huge group at the Hilton Hotel was a much different challenge.

Do I need someone to help me with a speech? I talked to my friends, and they told me to just be myself. I bought a small recorder at Staples. I wrote down things that had affected my life and made me what I am today. It took about twenty-five minutes.

I recorded my notes, and then I listened and made changes as needed.

When I did this, I truly looked at my life and the things that had most affected me. I had never done this before.

Amazingly, I was not nervous. My friends were concerned that I was not. I figured I had faced much bigger things in my life, and you just do the best you can.

Pam Marcus—I actually call her my adopted New York sister and dear friend—was only worried about what I was going to wear. For me, it's always best to wear what I feel like at the last minute. That is what I did.

I love to shop in resale shops, many times buying designer clothes that have never been worn or only slightly worn by women who evidently have nothing to do except shop. I pulled out a St. John (to some woman out there, I say thanks) from one of the shops. I paid thirty-five dollars for it.

Wearing that suit put me in the frame of mind that I needed to be in. I had been in the position of not being able to own such a suit. I was now able to but secure enough not to care that it had been owned by someone else.

They had a party to introduce us. The host was the charming Sally Minard, who has done so much for women's causes. I arrived and was surprised to be greeted by a man who asked me if I remembered him. He reminded me that I had donated trucks to a fund-raising event he had been involved with at Hemming + Gilman Productions five years earlier, and he told me that I was the only one who had ever donated a truck. Again, the importance of giving to good causes was reinforced.

Then Terry Lawler of New York Women in Film & Television, a woman whom I have known for years, greeted me. Although I do not have time to give on a daily basis, I have for a number of years given labor and trucks to move their yearly awards breakfast to the New York Hilton.

I was taken into a parlor to be introduced to the whole group of fifty or so along with the other Stars of 2006 Breakfast. The president of the agenda, Sandra Eberhard, asked me to sit with her. I was taken over to a down sofa to take the middle seat.

Wine glass in hand, I sat down. Of course, as life would have it, I was the first to be called for introduction.

I handed my glass to the next person and said, "Well, I can move almost anything in the city of New York as a trucker, and I do not know if I can move my ass out of this couch." Everyone laughed. Now all were at ease. I'm not sure how, but I pulled myself up and thanked all.

They told me I was to be the last speaker. I said, "Oh no." They said it was for good reason. Who was I to question further?

I sat on the dais and heard all these wonderful, successful women and said to myself, *You grew up in such a different world.* I had no degrees from great colleges, and I did not work for these great corporations.

I just had to be myself, and I was. I give you the transcript of the ceremony and the speech that helped me to write the book you have in hand.

Introduction

Rosanna Scotto, Fox 5 News Anchor Introduces Nadine Shelby Schramm (Star)

Scotto:

Our final star this morning is a truly extraordinary woman. Nadine Shelby Schramm is the president and CEO of Budd Enterprises Ltd., born in Charleston, Arkansas.

As an aside, I met Nadine a couple of nights ago at Elaine's. She works a crowd like a politician. Also, she stayed out later than me.

Nadine relocated to New York City and started her own business. It was her inherent will to succeed that led to the creation and success of several local businesses.

Later, it was her sharper business acumen that led her into the trucking business, taking over her husband's company after his death—the company was

Budd Enterprises Ltd.—then later starting a new company for the movie industry called Budd Leasing Ltd. Combined, they are now one of the leading theatrical trucking companies in the United States. Over the years, Budd Enterprises has supplied trucking and personnel to such important entertainment venues as CBS, the Metropolitan Opera and the New York Philharmonic's annual Concerts in the Parks, and the Macy's Thanksgiving Day Parade.

Nadine has continued with the company's expansion from seven to eighty-two trucks and obtained contracts with Radio City Music Hall to do all their labor for moves in and out of shows.

Although there were many, the ones early on were *The Sopranos* for all eight years, *Sex in the City*, and *Law and Order*. They were the beginnings in movies and television shows. She knew she had made a good decision to go that route.

An active member in the community, Nadine serves on the boards of many prestigious organizations, as well as her continual involvement with New York Women in Film & Television and the Actors Fund.

Nadine holds many of NYWA's initiatives to heart, including New York–based organization Breaking the Silence and her stance on domestic violence.

Given the opportunity, Nadine repeatedly encourages young people to rise above their own self-doubt and motivates them to start their own businesses. She is a steadfast leader in our ever-changing community.

Please welcome Nadine Shelby Schramm.

Schramm:

Thank you, Ms. Scotto.

And I want to thank NYWA for inviting me as an honoree today and Dr. Sal Cumella for nominating me to such a powerful women's organization.

I am truly honored.

I stand here today fully aware of the many people who have molded me into the person I am.

My mother and father, who so loved children that they had eleven.

My siblings and extended family, then my grandchildren Michael Salb, Kelly Nadine Salb, and Amanda Dianne Salb Tetreault, who are here today.

My father, was totally blind by the age of forty-five with retinitis pigmentosa, a hereditary disease, as was his mother and half my siblings as well as nieces and nephews—a total of fourteen.

There is no cure.

I have shared the above to let you know that I am eternally blessed with good sight, and with that came responsibility.

My father and mother taught us that *can't* should not be a word.

It has stuck with me.

By the age of twelve, weighing probably eighty pounds but with lots of muscle, I plowed the fields behind two horses each weighting sixteen hundred pounds.

My father walked with me and held the reins and one hand on the plow for safety in case the horses were spooked.

I felt so lucky because I had my dad's attention all to myself.

I learned so much from him. He is still the smartest man I have ever known.

He received recordings from the federal government, so he had the latest newspapers, magazines, and books all read and recorded by actors, people we never saw.

Little did I know I would someday meet many of the great voices of the day.

My first husband was an abuser, both physically and mentally.

I stayed much too long out of fear as many do. But I did survive, and I became a much stronger person.

I started my first business. I had gained my confidence and respect back.

I was free.

I wanted to do so many things. I started five businesses and loved each one for different reasons.

Then I met Bud Schramm in a business meeting and remember thinking how lucky some woman was to have him as a husband, only to find he was in divorce proceedings.

He was different. He was a true gentleman. I married him three years later, total bliss for twenty-three years. And then I lost him suddenly of a massive heart attack on December 23, 1990.

My world drastically changed in those few minutes.

I gave up my business, sat down in Bud's chair, and became president of Budd Enterprises and never thought of the word *can't*.

I did not do it alone. Tom O'Donnell, president of Theatrical Teamsters Local 817, never questioned my ability.

The members, many of whose grandfathers, fathers, and uncles have worked for the Schramm family since the late 1800s, gave me the opportunity to work with them as a trucker.

I have great respect for them. It must have been hard for them to think I could handle it.

Well, remember the Teamster emblem? It has two horse heads in the middle, and I had followed horses before.

We have customers who have been with us for years, many who are here today.

I still marvel at the opportunities that are there if you take the road available to you.

It has been a wonderful trip from that farm in Arkansas to the world I live in today.

If there is anyone in the room today who is abused, walk. It does not get better. Only worse.

If there are persons whose dreams they are afraid to pursue, fear of failure is the only thing that can stop you.

In closing, *can't* should not be in your vocabulary.

I thank all of you for being here and supporting NYWA.

Have a wonderful holiday season with health, happiness, and love.

Thank you.

In the '70s, people started telling me I should write a book. I had a business by the name of Unfinished Business, which repaired and refinished antique furniture and then also brownstone woodwork.

I continued to get the message from friends, and I always have given a flip answer: "I'm not finished yet." Well, my first speech was at the New York Hilton to a large women's organization.

My speech at New York Women's Agenda (comprised of one hundred thousand businesswomen) made people cry, laugh and then I received a standing ovation. It was their first standing ovation in sixteen years. Partly because of this reaction, I am now writing this book, *Unfinished Business*.

That was the first time I'd spoken to an audience, and afterward, it felt as if it were almost an out-of-body experience.

I had no idea of the impact it would have, and when people stood and clapped and cheered, I was quite shocked.

A line of people formed afterward to talk to me and shake my hand, and several women were in tears saying they were going to change their own lives by making needed changes.

A mother and daughter in tears were in line, and the mother told me her daughter said to her while I was speaking, "Mom, if she could do it in her time, I am making the changes in my life I have needed to do for some time."

I realized if I could have that effect and if I touched fifteen hundred people, with many expressing how I had given the inspiration to do anything they wanted and not fear failure, and then I should write that book and inspire many others.

CHAPTER 1

My Childhood; A Farmer's Daughter

Born on January 19, I am a true Capricorn—stubborn as can be when I believe in something. It has helped in many ways because I never quit a project. If you doubt that, I will show you how no matter how long it takes.

My journey began on a small farm outside Branch, Arkansas. The closest larger city is Fort Smith on the Oklahoma border. I was one of eleven children. Our mother and father made each of us feel special for different reasons.

All the generations in our family are close; we believe that, together, we are strong. Nieces and nephews and their mates and children now carry on the creed of my mother and father. We never fight or try to control one another.

We kid each other, and it is always in good fun. No one wants to leave the room, because when you come back in, everyone sits quietly for a minute to let you know you could have been the object of chatter. No one gets offended. Do not pick on one of us, or you will deal with us all. We never tell each other what to do. We make our own decisions and live by them with support from everyone.

We make telephone companies happy, because if there is illness or good times, we all talk to one another. In two days, the word is spread. Everyone gets updates daily until things have gotten back to normal.

Never have I been bored at any time in my life. I always say, "I came in laughing, and I hope I go the same way."

I always remember the story of my mom, Gussie Lee Brown, and dad, Hobart McKinley Shelby—nicknamed Kin—getting married and the decisions they had to make.

Daddy knew he had the same eye problem, retinitis pigmentosa, that his mother had and that he would lose his sight as she did at an early age.

They had another obstacle to their plans, since World War I had started, and Daddy was of age. He had to wait and see if he would be called. He was called, but the army would not take him because of his eyesight. It was already too bad. I have the papers that he was turned down.

He was in college studying finance. He knew that without sight, finance was not to be his calling, although he loved it. So they decided to become farmers. My mother grew up on a farm. Daddy grew up with a father who was a Baptist minister.

What a leap they took to become farmers. But he became a very good one. There were many obstacles to overcome, but they worked together, and it is amazing how they overcame so many.

I was born the sixth child of eleven.

We were such a happy family and did not think anything of our work schedule. Actually, it was good for us, because we all grew up with good work ethics.

Never did we hear loud voices from our mother or father. This did not mean there was no discipline. There were ten children—after a twin died at six months—and my parents were always there ... and usually our friends or cousins too. It was like a party to kids who might not have brothers or sisters or who just had a small family.

The first thing I remember as a child was my dad having pneumonia.

At that time, they did not know if it was infectious. We were not allowed in the room. My mother went in and out. Dr. Bollinger came. He was the only doctor in the area. He was paid mostly in eggs, chickens, vegetables, and sometimes pork or beef. No one had money. This was during the Great Depression of the '30s.

There were no antibiotics. The doctor finally told my mother there was nothing else he could do. My father was probably not going to live.

The doctor brought out a bottle of liquor that was homemade, called white lightning. He told my mother that Dad had to drink it. They were not drinkers, but that bottle saved his life. The fever that had been raging broke. He was drenched with perspiration. That was exactly what the doctor wanted.

Daddy was weak for many months but survived. I could not have been more than three. Maybe that's the reason I enjoy my scotch and soda in a wine glass.

Dr. Bollinger was a country doctor who came for all our births in the home. My maternal grandmother assisted, because doctors did not have nurses then. It had to be difficult on everyone. The doctor could not always be there because others were sometimes in need at the same time. He would arrive as soon as possible.

My birth certificate was not filed until two years after I was born. I reminded Dr. Bollinger of this in his later years and kidded him that he could not keep up with my mom and dad. He told me they were just as excited with the last as with the first. I told him they were just as happy with grandchildren and great-grandchildren. Twice we have had five generations living.

I became sick with a very high fever when I was young. I am not sure, but I think it was scarlet fever. I was in a baby bed. I was shaking very badly. I said to my mother, "I think I am going to die." I had seen my little sister die.

At that young age, I guess we all were afraid we would be next. My mother told me later when we talked about it that she thought I was going to die too.

Another early memory is of our house burning. We lived on a farm outside Charleston, Arkansas. It was a school day, and therefore only my younger brother and I were home with our mother.

Daddy and our neighbors were baling hay. They always helped each other, as it was heavy work, cutting with a mower pulled by horses and then baling by hand. My mother was ironing clothes with an iron heated on a wood cookstove.

I begged her to take us to the barn to get peanuts. We were there for a while. All of a sudden, she realized from the smell of smoke that the house was on fire. She grabbed us up and put us in a little house; I think a chicken house or an outhouse. If you do not know what that is, it is an outdoor toilet. We got out and followed her into the house.

She panicked. She took us out with the few clothes she had been ironing. That is the extent of what was saved. All family pictures—not to mention furniture, clothes, bedding, and so on—were destroyed.

My father and the other men saw the house burning and raced in their wagons. There was of course no water except from the well. They grabbed bucket after bucket, but it was futile. The house was gone.

I remember seeing my mother and father hugging and crying. They had lost everything.

When the school bus came, there was no home. My oldest brother, Ralph, had just gotten a new pair of shoes. He had a sore foot, so he had only worn one shoe to school that day. He cried because his other shoe was gone.

The neighbors took us into their homes—some of us to different ones. Then our parents found a house for us to all move to. People gave a plate, a bowl, or whatever they could, but these were Depression years, and no one had much. The banker, Mr. Haitt, gave a quarter.

I have the list of items each family gave. My parents were just happy no one was hurt.

I was four when the twins were born. Their names were Martha Sue and Mary Lou; their first names were of our grandmothers. At six months, Mary Lou became ill with pneumonia and intestinal flu. Again, there were no antibiotics, and she passed away quickly.

Her death was another of my early memories. When she died, there were no funeral homes in the county.

The funerals were always in the home or church. I remember my grandmother covering what we called a library table with a white cloth and then laying the baby on it.

A neighbor, Ott Dow, came in and put pennies on her eyelids to keep them closed. My mother and father were devastated. They loved their children so, and it was rare to have twins in those days. It is such a vivid memory.

Two years later, my mother gave birth to Neta Fern. My mother always said she looked exactly like Mary Lou. Although Martha was only six months at Mary Lou's death, she always said she felt half of her was missing.

Our mother made paper patterns from looking at the Sears catalog and then used flour sacks—which, in those days, were printed cotton—to make our dresses.

She could have been in the fashion industry. None of our friends had such individual clothing made on a Singer treadle sewing machine.

One day, I decided I would do some sewing when she was distracted. I put my little hand right in front of the needle on the cloth and started pedaling away right over my finger. There I was screaming with the needle though my middle finger. All she had to do was one turn on the little side wheel, and out the needle came.

I did not try to sew again until I was an adult, but for many years, I could see a little black spot where the needle had gone through.

I remember my first piece of clothing bought ready-made, as the saying went, when I was eight years old. It was a beautiful grape-colored coat with a velvet collar. It was ordered from the Sears & Roebuck catalog.

It came by mail, and I was so excited. But it rained the first day as I walked to meet the school bus. Rain was pouring down, and so was the color running down my legs.

The coat was ruined, and I cried when my mother said it had to go back. I do not remember if I got a replacement. It could never have had the effect on me that getting that first one did.

Our mother was always doing a dozen things at a time with so many children. She had to sew, clean, wash clothes by hand, and keep us safe. People complain that they have to do laundry. Try doing it in an iron pot set up over a pile of burning wood with homemade lye soap, boiling the clothes and then scrubbing them on a metal board. We had germ-free clothing, clean beyond what you have today. The water all had to be drawn from the well.

She also helped in the fields and made a garden. I think the time she spent on her flower garden was the time she took for her enjoyment. She grew the most beautiful roses and many other flowers from cuttings of others. I always think of my mother with the roses she grew.

All of us felt special for different reasons. Every picture of us is strictly by age. Inez, the oldest, got to where she tried to sneak out of line. We never let her. Over the years, she felt like our boss, and we let her. Then we did what we wanted.

During and after the Depression, we had many hobos come to our farm looking for food. Hobos were the equivalent of today's homeless. They rode freight trains from Chicago and other large towns, riding mostly on the top for free by getting on in the dark and then getting off in small towns, looking for work and food.

We were a large family living in the Depression years. Think of *The Grapes of Wrath* by John Steinbeck. It is a great book, and if you have not read it, you should to understand what this country came back from. It's funny that John Steinbeck lived on North Haven but died shortly before I lived there. However, the Schramm family saw him many times.

The crops burned because there was no rain. There were no jobs anywhere, so the hobos begged. They came, and my mother would hand them food through the back door. They could sit in the shade on the porch to eat. She always shared what she could and kept a big metal pan of breakfast rolls and cookies ready, as well as a jug of iced tea. They were all very thankful.

Daddy had a rule, though: she had to hand the food out to them; he never allowed them in the house. He simply felt that maybe one of them might not be honorable.

Daddy would let them sleep in the barn on the hay with the promise never to smoke inside it. It must have been difficult for him knowing what fires could and did do with our house having been burned to the ground.

Never did one give any trouble. My parents felt very sorry for them and told us to always be respectful, but we were always told to stay in the house.

Radio was the way to keep up with news on a daily basis. It was on a few hours per day. I remember my first big experience with radio. Daddy loved to hear the prize fights with Joe Louis and all the others. Joe was the biggest draw. The big fight of the day was with Joe Louis and Schmeling on June 2, 1938.

The morning of the fight there was a huge storm, and lightning came in on the radio wires from the pole outside our house. It was a Philco radio that stood about four feet high by two feet.

The lightning blew it into matchsticks. It set the drapes on fire. Thank goodness they put the fire out. This was the morning before that fight in the evening.

The lightning went through the house. How it did not kill any of us I will never know. Ralph was lying on a bed with metal springs, and it went through the springs. Ralph was frozen for a few minutes and said he could not move.

It's funny I remember the lightning streaking through like a long string of fire.

What to do about the prize fight? Daddy took me

with him to our neighbors that night, and his eyesight was mostly gone. I do not know how many miles it was. It was a long walk, and without a doubt, it took longer than my father thought it would because I was slower than he was.

We walked in the door just to hear the roar of the crowd. Joe Lewis had a technical knockout in the first round. I think that fight lasted maybe two minutes. I am sure that it was a long walk home for my father. He had missed the big fight.

Annette, the sister two years older than I am, learned to tap dance when she was very young, and I have never seen anyone, including all the ones I've seen in movies and Broadway, that could move his or her feet as fast as she could. You could hardly see her feet; they were like a blur. The teachers were always putting her in talent shows at school. They would black her face; in all probability, they thought only black people could dance like that.

I did not know how she learned, and later, I asked her. She said she never saw anyone; it just came to her when she was very young. Maybe it came from a past life.

I never saw anyone else ever tap until years later. We could sometimes get her to tap for the younger generation at one of our family reunions.

Her eyesight was even bad when she was young, and her health was not good, either. As a youngster, I did not understand why she was always too sick to work the fields. In fact, I sometimes just thought she was lazy or just hated farming.

She was smart and always earned straight *A*s or *A*+s. She was valedictorian of her class.

When people were really sick and many times on their deathbeds, the neighbors would sit with families so they would not be alone during long sickness or deathwatch. One night, Daddy and another man were sitting, and it was a long, tough night. There was an old maid sister who lived in the house.

The people told them there was a bed they could use to take turns for a little sleep. The other guy decided to take a break, and he went right into what he thought was the correct bedroom. Lo and behold, there was no light, and he climbed in with the old maid. She started screaming. He ran out. He had left his clothes on, so it was just so funny. Daddy would tell the story and laugh so hard many years later.

We never went to bed hungry, and the relatives all came to our house for Sunday dinners. They rarely had our family over to their houses. They always said they could not handle that many and said, "Well, it's easier for Aunt Gussie; she knows how to cook for a crowd." And crowd it was, usually twenty to thirty people.

That meant more than a one-gallon bucket of potatoes, three to four fried chickens, and all kinds of vegetables. Her pies were absolutely the best. We still use her recipes for banana cream, chocolate, coconut cream, and lemon meringue. The cobblers of peach or apple with her biscuit dough were the best.

We all shared our recipes. Neta put together a cookbook of Shelby family recipes, and it brings back memories. Funny, but they do not taste exactly like Mama's.

My sisters and I did not think these Sundays were fair from our viewpoint, because we had to wash all the dishes while our cousins were in the yard playing.

Daddy had a horse called Ole Sleepy that no one could ride except him. That horse looked and walked like a Tennessee walking horse. One day, he and our mother had gone into town to do major shopping, and my younger brother Jim and a neighbor boy named Frank Owens and I—all three of us under twelve years old—decided we would ride Ole Sleepy. We got his bridle and somehow got it on him and took him over to a bale of hay so we could get on. Surprisingly, we mounted him.

We were in the barnyard that was fenced in, and Sleepy took off, and up he went over the fence. As Sleepy jumped over and started down, off we went. How he did not step on us is still amazing to me.

Now Sleepy was out and running as fast as he could with the bridle on. We tried but of course could not get him back into the barn area.

When our parents got home, the first thing Daddy did was go to the barn to take his ride, only to find Sleepy on the other side of the fence. He whistled for him, and Sleepy came. But there was one problem. Why was Sleepy wearing the bridle?

He asked us. We were very quiet and very scared. I could never lie to my parents, so I told the truth. I know my father almost had a heart attack knowing all of us could easily have been killed. But as usual, there was no loud shouting or whipping—just a sit-down and talk that hurt more than any belt.

We never rode Sleepy again.

We did get to ride the plow horses, and they never seemed to care. They were very used to us in the fields, and we were a lot lighter than the plows they pulled day after day. Daddy was always with us on these rides, though, just for our safety.

I had the experience of having my younger sister Martha, who was ten years old, cut herself while peeling an apple when our parents had gone to town to do shopping. I was the oldest at home. She was bleeding badly, and I knew I had to get her to the doctor, so I took her to the neighbors' house to ask them to take us.

The doctor told me I would have to hold her arm, as he did not have a nurse. He started sewing, and I really felt sorry for my sister, and she was crying. I told him that I thought I was going to faint. He sternly said, "No, you are not." I closed my eyes but did not turn loose of her.

I still say my father was one of the smartest men I have ever known. He received from the Library of Congress recordings for the blind free; he had all the books, magazines, and newspapers of the day read and recorded by actors with those wonderful voices. My father ordered these records, and they came in large bundles every week or so. We had a Victrola player. We kids got to wind it up, and then we all listened. Otherwise, the noise was rather heavy with all of the talking and laughing.

We learned a lot about things that most kids did not hear about in those days, including all the speeches by politicians. Even our teachers did not have access to all of that.

He received those recordings until he died, and he so enjoyed them, and of course, my mother was always there. Little did I know that I would someday meet many actors with voices like the ones I heard from those recordings.

I wish all children could live on a farm for a few years. You learn so much just in the everyday work schedules. Cows have to be milked every morning and night. Before the school bus comes and then after school, you go to work in the fields, and you milk again at night; there is no putting it off. Then you do your homework. The grass grows in the fields, and it must be cut, or you grow no food. You have to harvest the food on time, or it rots. In other words, there is no excuse or saying, "I will do it tomorrow." Tomorrow is also a day of work.

We also learned about birthing, as it was just a routine of the farm. There was little time to get into trouble. We used to pray for rain so we could have a day of play.

I was not a very good student. Annette, two years older than I, made straight As. Jim, just younger, seemed to never open a book and made such grades they pushed him up a class. Well, it was celebration time when I made a *B+*. My teachers as well as my mother and father thought I could do better.

I always had the excuse that I liked so many things and that they only liked books. I was always busy. I was never bored and spent a lot of time with boys in my class. I guess I was more of a tomboy, as they included me always. I didn't think anything of it; I just liked the more rugged things. Now I understand why.

Daddy needed a boy to help him, and I loved being the chosen one. A girl who could do anything a boy would do. He taught me how to plow the fields when I was ten or twelve and was always by my side. I loved it and could cut very close to the plants, and it saved many hours of hoeing the grass left close to the corn, cotton, or whatever else we were growing. Several of the nearby farmers would wait until I was finished with ours and then hire me to plow theirs. They did not discriminate against a female.

Do not think I did not know I was good. I never disliked the hard labor. It meant maybe a dollar a day to go to family needs. Those were very special times for me.

I loved basketball and social life. I look back and realize that even at that young age I was always ready to join in on any sport, and no matter how rough and tumble, I could hold my own.

We all had so much fun, and it was an important part of our lives learning how to share wins and losses.

I have a cousin my age named Gwendolyn Brown Vest, and she was a great basketball player and always scored more than the rest of us. She was big for her age, and she would go down court and stand close to the goal and just lay up shot after shot. No one could cover her. I was always much less in weight compared to my classmates, but I was tough. I was fast on the basketball court, and our team won many games. I was not afraid to push for a goal anytime I had a chance. It was about the only diversion we had from schoolwork or the farm.

We went by school bus to other towns to play

basketball, and I will tell you we were pretty tough, but there were some games after which we were not so happy on the bus coming home. There was one school in Mountain Home, Arkansas, which was up in the mountain area, and those girls had bodies taller and bigger than their brothers. We did not ever beat them; we just felt lucky to come home healthy.

We did have school activities like contests to raise money. We had beauty contests and would sell tickets, and whoever raised the most money was crowned queen.

I was in the contest once, and our neighbors' daughter was in it too. It was at the Halloween party held each year. Their family had more than ours, so she was winning, but my sister Gladys was dating a naval recruiting officer whom she later married, and he started giving for me.

Well, the night of the decision, it was very close and getting a little testy, so they decided there would be two queens. We took turns wearing the crown. It was all in good fun, as far as I was concerned.

It was and is important for me to spend time with friends, and in the summer, we had house parties with games like spin the bottle, which kids of today probably have not heard of. All girls stand in a circle in a yard, and a boy spins a bottle. Whoever it stopped in front of had to take a walk with him down a dirt road. We all lived on farms, so we met on different ones. Well, if you had nothing else, this was fun, and it led to many becoming daters.

In the Depression years, my uncle Leon Brown had left Arkansas, but he sold three heifers and bought new tires for his Ford Model T. He later told of how many cars he saw broken down. He made it to California and got work on a ranch up in the mountains. He slept in barns at night. The mountain lions came to the barnyard after the cattle during the night. He was scared to death of being eaten alive by a mountain lion and said he was more afraid of them than the guns he would encounter during the war.

World War II broke out shortly after he got there. He was one of the first called. He received two weeks of training and went through the whole war as an infantryman. He knew mechanics and kept the tanks running. They went by foot all through the war across Europe fighting the Germans. He was one of the first landing in and one of the last out, clothes in rags and boots worn out. He arrived home shell shocked.

In all those years, there was no communication. I was very young, but I remember Daddy and Grandpa Brown picking him up by wagon in Branch, Arkansas, when he was discharged. There was great excitement in the family, but what a sad sight. He was lying in the back of the wagon all curled up. Daddy and Grandpa spent many nights just sitting with him, not talking, and letting him know he was loved. There were no doctors then to treat them for the trauma of war. Our families never even hunted animals.

There were never guns in our homes, and to see what they could do to a human being was horrible. He would never talk about it. He had been to hell and back. But the war was won with much credit going to American soldiers. It was a just war, but many soldiers died for many others to live.

My father, my grandfather, and my uncle Wayne sat up all nights with Uncle Leon to make sure he was okay. He hardly said a word. He slowly gained back weight and strength and more so started talking, and soon he was thinking of what he wanted to do after about one year.

He started a little business in Fort Smith repairing cars. He did this all his life and became very successful. He was very short, and he met a wonderful young woman who was also very petite, whom he married. They loved to dance and also were very good. She wore a size-three shoe and had to buy a child's shoe and later got samples that fit. They had lots of fun.

He had a long, hard time getting back to normal after the hell he went through during that war.

CHAPTER 2

My World Turned Upside Down

My parents had given up the farm when I graduated high school. I was the last to be able to do the plowing as the brother just younger than I was had no love of the farm, and then two girls younger could not. The time had come for my father and mother to slow down.

When my parents moved into town, Daddy could now walk to my uncle's store, Brown's Dry Goods, by himself every day at 10:00 a.m. We always laughed and said you could set your watch by Daddy's trip to get a Coke. Uncle Wayne and Aunt Bonetta Brown owned the only dry goods store for miles around, and they also had a telephone, so everybody used it to make calls. People could buy almost anything they needed at that store, including fabric, food, and farm items. Kids especially loved going there, as they had a candy counter enclosed in glass. They could buy penny candy or trade one egg for a few pieces.

Daddy had always done most of the shopping for all

supplies. Mama would sit down and tell him what she needed, but she never wrote it down for him. Daddy rarely forgot anything from her long lists of items. Blindness never deterred him from having a fairly regular life.

He also knew what money he had. When he took money from the bank, Mr. Hiatt, the banker, would put the bills in order by denomination for him. Daddy knew how many ones, fives, and tens he had and would remember what he spent and exactly which bills he still had. He did not need a bank statement, and back then, no one got those, anyway.

Aunt Bonetta was beautiful, and she and Daddy loved to talk and tell jokes. She was always coming over to see our parents, and one day, my mother was out in the backyard when Aunt Bonetta had come in and was in the kitchen. She was getting a drink of water at the sink with her back to my father when he walked in. Daddy thought it was Mama at the sink, so he walked over and gave her butt a squeeze. Bonetta started to laugh and said, "It's not Gussie."

Remember, he was blind.

Of course, the joke was on him, but he turned it. He said, "Well, I always wanted to do that." My mother loved telling that story.

It's a good thing it was not the widow who had a habit

of showing up often. I think she had a crush on Daddy, and I can understand—he was handsome.

Now I will share the beginning of my life in 1952 as an abused woman and the explanation of the Texan mentioned before.

When I was eighteen in 1948 and had started to work at Dixie Cup, my girlfriends and I always met on Sundays to have a bite to eat and catch a movie when we did not have dates.

One Sunday, a girl I had gone to school with and who also worked at Dixie Cup and I were at Porta's, a drive-in and restaurant where we all hung out. In came two soldiers—one was very handsome and the other ugly as sin.

They sat next to us, and the good-looking one started talking to my friend and asked us to go to another drive-in. I said no and that we were on our way to a movie. She wanted to go, and I knew they were soldiers, but I relented and said that we would go only if we were brought back in time to go as scheduled.

We went out, and there sat a beautiful Buick convertible. Most soldiers did not even have cars but rode army buses into town. He was also dressed better than most. We did not go to the movie, and I was not happy. She went out with him three or four times, but she said he kept asking for my number.

I told her not to give it to him under any circumstances, but she got tired of the hassle he gave her and finally gave it to him. Now I had a big problem, because I would not go out with him. He showed up every night when I got off work. My friends and I always rode a bus back to downtown together.

It was really embarrassing to me. I thought if I went out with him once, he would see that I was not what he was looking for.

He took me back to my apartment and walked me to the door. I could not wait to get my key in the door. As I opened it, he shoved me inside. I lived with my sister Annette, and I hoped she was home, but instead, she was out with friends.

My life changed drastically in 1952.

It is still very hard for me to tell this part of my story, as it is very vivid to this day. He raped me although I was a very strong person. I had done the work of a man all though my childhood. I fought for probably thirty to forty-five minutes, praying that Annette would come home.

Then I became so tired and also now scared for my life, and he was an animal. I still think he may have killed if he had not won his pursuit. I never had any trouble with anyone like that before, and a no was always taken as no.

Then he started to threaten me if I told anyone. That

night when he left, I showered, got in bed, and pretended I was asleep when Annette came home.

I did not sleep that night or many to come.

I was so ashamed, scared, and humiliated, and I was afraid I might be pregnant. I was, but I soon had a miscarriage. I was a wreck. Report him to the police? I did not even think of it because of my pride and humiliation and now fear. I had fought but lost.

How could this have happened to me? He knew I wanted no part of him. But he was constant like a shadow. My sister hated him from the day she met him. He was around now all the time, and the threats became very intense.

I had gone from a very happy person to looking like a deer in headlights. I felt soiled by a man I did not even know. I was afraid to tell Annette or anyone else, because then they would be in the same scary place I was. Of course, that played right into his plans. If only I had gone to any of my young male friends I am sure would have taken care of him. Shame prevailed, and I was isolated for a long time.

He was what is called a stalker today from Houston, Texas. He had me so scared. He actually took me to a justice of the peace in a little town called Van Buren, and he married me under an assumed name—Lanier. His real name was Alten, a shortened form of a much longer Greek name. Why did he want marriage?

I found out he used an assumed name. He had that car, a big Buick convertible. He ended up in the base camp hospital with ulcers. He had left the car with me, but it was never for me to drive.

Then he wanted me to bring the car out to where he was being treated, which of course I was going to do, as I had no doubt about what I would go through if I did not. The car would not start, so I tried to call him at the hospital. They said there was no one there by that name. I insisted. I knew I would be in deep trouble otherwise. He was in the army at the time, stationed in Camp Chaffee, Arkansas. He told me that he was also an officer with the CIA.

He was a very handsome Greek-Irish man with olive skin and black hair, and he had an unusual car for a soldier. They knew exactly who he was, and he was there.

The doctor said, "I have someone you need to talk to."

I said, "Okay."

It turned out to be a chaplain. He said, "We know who you are asking for. That is not his name, and if you are married under the name Lanier and he says he is a CIA agent, then he has federal charges against him. He is not, and you have to file the charges. Also, I think you are in danger."

Now I knew I was in much more trouble than I had

imagined, and I was really freaked. I did not take the car out. Instead, two CIA agents came to see me. Of all places, they came to my workplace. Now it was very unusual to have such authorities visit.

They wanted me to sign papers and said to not be afraid and that he would go away for years. Embarrassed and really freaked out, I said, "I can sign nothing until I see my parents."

My poor mother and father—what a mess I had brought to them. My father said, "Nadine, do not press charges. He will get out, and you will always be his target for turning him in. He will be discharged and go out of town. You can get an annulment."

I did not tell my parents of the death threats. It was too much for me to even utter to these wonderful but naive people who never knew violence.

How unprepared we all were to deal with him.

He did not leave me alone. He really became impossible and threatened my life and again my family. I was a mess. How could my life change so drastically in such a short time?

I did not press charges; therefore, they could do nothing. I was the only witness and with papers. He was discharged; I am sure it was a dishonorable discharge, although I never saw papers.

I knew my dad thought he was giving good advice, but how could he possibly know how to handle it? He never knew violence, so he did not know what to do except to hope he would leave.

Tom came to the apartment where we were living and told me, "Pack your bags; we are leaving." I asked where we were going, and he told me that we were going to Youngstown, Ohio, where his father and stepmother lived.

I went thinking that at least I could protect my parents.

I found out when we got there that he had not seen his father since he was very young and that his mother had divorced his father and moved to Texas.

We lived with them for some time. I knew no one, and he liked it that way because he did not have to worry so much of what I might do.

He carried a briefcase that was always locked, and one night, he was really agitated, and he wanted me to do something against my will. I do not remember what, as he was always making demands, but I was saying no.

I have blocked many things from my mind for survival, and this is one.

He pulled a small pistol out of the briefcase and put it to my head. I laughed and said, "Oh, it's a toy." He took the cylinder out, and it was missing one bullet. He said,

"Which one do you think it would be—the empty or the bullet?"

I got a job working in a hotel as a desk clerk. I enjoyed working there, as it meant time away and with normal people. My hours were the same as Tom's, so he would drop me off and pick me up. Good control always.

He did work as a machinist when we were in Ohio, and he must have been good, as he kept the job for some time. It was so different from the way he was most of the time in the way he dressed and all other aspects. He said he had learned that trade as a youngster.

We were living in Youngstown, Ohio, when my daughter was born in 1954. We had rented a house sometime after I became pregnant. The day she was born, he threw a plate of pasta on the kitchen wall, and I scrubbed it off. What a mess.

The night I went into labor, he drove me to the hospital and left me. It was my due date. He did not come to the hospital after dropping me off. His father was very nice to me and came every day to see his granddaughter. He was Greek and brought his friends up to see us.

I was lucky that I had a very easy pregnancy with little morning sickness and gained only twelve pounds for a seven-pound-three-ounce baby. I had no problem taking off that little gain. You could hardly tell I was pregnant until the last two months.

Tom then came to take us home. I was in the hospital for a week, which was the normal time back then. He had come into the hospital and named her Mary Anne without my knowledge after his mother and sister. I had not even met them. I tried to get them to change it, but they said no because it had been filed with the state.

Isolated from all my friends and family, I felt so alone, and I had a new problem—keeping my baby safe. I was so happy I had someone to love and who needed me.

When she was three weeks old, he was really at his worst, screaming and so angry. I was afraid he would hurt my child, and I ran out of the house in a nightgown with Mary Anne in a baby blanket, as this all happened when I was giving her a bath. I got her into the car. Thank God the key was in it. He came out and beat on the car as I backed out of the driveway. I had locked the doors.

I went to the police station and walked in, telling them that I wanted to file a complaint against my husband. They asked my name and address. I told them, and all of a sudden, the officer told me to wait. He went into the back and then returned and said, "You will have to come back tomorrow to file the complaint. Do you have someplace to spend the night?"

I said, "No, I am from Arkansas, and I have no family or friends here."

He said, "No relatives?"

I said, "His uncle and aunt or father, but I cannot go there; he will come there first looking for me."

He said, "Go there; you will be safe with them."

Of course, Tom came there. Back I went. It took me many years later to figure out why the police at that station did not want to bring charges. It was because of Tom's uncle's Mafia connections.

The uncle owned a Greek coffeehouse. No women allowed.

Every afternoon, two burly-looking men went to the uncle's house with an old calculator that made loud noises. They went into a back room with the uncle and spent a couple of hours on the machine and then left with it.

Years later, I figured out they must have been the Greek Mafia with the numbers games. A Greek coffeehouse and counting money in a back room? No doubt not your normal business. Boy, was I naive. I did not even know there was such a thing as the Mafia. Why would I?

Their name was sure recognized at that police station, and they were not about to arrest a nephew. It must have been a good payoff. Glad I did not know until years later. I was already beaten down enough.

My mother and sister Annette and a young man she was dating drove to Ohio to see us.

Mary Anne was three months old. Tom had such anger when she cried that I rocked her all night every night so he would not take it out on me.

My mother heard me up all night for three nights rocking, and as she was leaving, she said to me, "Nadine, you can come home anytime. Do not forget this; you do not have to live this way."

CHAPTER 3

Ups And Downs of Getting my Life Back Together

My brother-in-law Mike Devito, my older sister Inez's husband, was driving to Arkansas from New York a few weeks later. I made arrangements for him to pick me up on the way at a small motel on the interstate on the outskirts of Youngstown, Ohio.

My father-in-law took me there. He had seen Tom treat me terribly many times, but he did not know what to do, and he was of small stature, and Tom was big and strong.

I stayed there two days until Mike arrived to pick us up.

My father-in-law hid me and brought milk for Mary and food for me for those days. He was always very kind to me, and I know he was very upset with what I was going through.

What a trip, and what an angel Mike was to do this. We drove all the way without stopping for the nights, and it was hot. There was no air conditioner in the car, and it was over one hundred degrees in Missouri.

We bought watermelon for moisture; there was no bottled water then. Cars were not air-conditioned back then. I really do not know how we made it. It was really a rough ride even for adults and me with a baby.

I went to live with my mother and father, and I went back to work at Dixie Cup, this time in the office.

When I walked in to visit Mr. Kingsnorth, head of the operation in Fort Smith, he called me into his office and said, "Are you visiting or back to stay?"

I told him that I was there to stay and that I was looking for a job.

He said, "You have one here," and he called the office manager in and said, "Give Nadine a job in the office."

I drove back and forth seventeen miles each way. My brother Ralph bought me an old Buick car for $300. It took me a while, but I paid him back.

My mother and father took care of Mary Anne while I worked.

We were doing just fine. One problem was that Mary never wanted to sleep for long periods of time. She would sleep off and on all day long.

Daddy, who had taken care of so many babies, would sit and rock her, knowing I needed to get some rest so I could be at work at 9:00 a.m. with an hour's drive. He would think he had her asleep and would bring her into my bed, and in a few minutes, the crying would start.

I would get up and rock her, and she would always want to be held up on my chest. The little squirt would reach up and pull on my lashes to make sure I was awake. At such a young age, she had things figured out.

Daddy said he had never had a child he could not put to sleep. He was a hands-on father and did help all the time with all us kids. He considered it as much his job as our mother's. He always seemed so happy with two or three kids piled on his lap. Well, Mary was one who bested him.

I would take her to the young doctor who had started a practice in Charleston after Dr. Bollinger had retired. He was very busy, but the nurse and he would have me bring Mary to the back door and sneak us in and play with her. She really was a beautiful baby with black curly hair and black eyes, and she knew how to get attention. He would play for longer, and I felt guilty because there were so many sick people out front waiting. He could never find a thing wrong with her. She was healthy. I think it was all caused by the fact I was always so nervous and upset when I was carrying her that it affected her. Or maybe she just took after her father, as he never slept much at night, and that is when he was his meanest.

I was happy living with my parents, but it was a strain on them, and knew I should be on my own, so I moved to Fort Smith. Now I could get more rest without that long drive every day.

Money was tight. I had to hire a babysitter and was lucky that a woman with two children lived in the apartment complex where I rented. She charged little, but she needed money as badly as I did. It was not a very nice place—it was a small, second-floor place, and it was unbelievably hot in the summer with no air-conditioning, but I was happy.

A woman who was the office manager at Dixie Cup talked down to all of us and was plain mean more to others than to me. They were upset every day. They asked me to speak to her. I asked her to go to the ladies' room with me. I told her she was making everyone miserable, and in my mind, it was unacceptable.

To me, she was just another bully. I did not like it and thought I might also be the one who should tell her—me, the one who needed the job more than others. But I had been toughened.

She said, "Am I really that bad?" I said yes. She thanked me for telling her and said she would change. She did, and I got thanks from all.

I got a better job at the Arkansas Medical Society with a few dollars more in pay. It was very interesting to me. We kept all records of doctors in the state and sent out information on them and handled requests of people looking for specialists and so on.

I got a notice from a lawyer that Tom wanted a divorce. Well, so did I, but I did not have money for a lawyer, so just as long as he stayed away, I was okay.

I had Dale Bumpers, who later became governor and then a senator, get my divorce for me. All I asked for was full custody—no alimony or support ... just freedom.

Good riddance.

Dale knew my circumstances, and when I ask for a bill, he said, "It's $7.50."

I said, "No, the real price—it may take me a while to pay it all."

He said, "No, that is the price. It pays for paper and the secretary's time." He got what I wanted.

I thought I was the only one Dale did this for and that I was special, but Betty, his wife, told me much later that he did more work for free than he ever charged for.

There were only three of us in that small medical records office, and I was a divorced woman with a child. The man in charge was married with no children, and the other was a mousy young woman who, as far I could tell, did not date. We never had much conversation; it was just work, which was fine with me. They did not want to hear about children, and that was my life.

We went to a medical convention in Little Rock, and we each had separate rooms. I would have been fine to share with my coworker, as I grew up with six sisters and always shared bedrooms. Well, the first night, I figured we would all go to dinner, or at least she and I would.

I mentioned having dinner, and she said, "Oh, I am just going to grab a sandwich and eat it in my room." It was not a nice attitude, but that was not unusual for her. Later, I found out the reason for her excuse.

Our expenses were paid for, so I went alone to have a good dinner. This is before my brother and family had moved to Little Rock.

Time went on, and I thought things were fine; I had no complaints. I did my work, and I enjoyed it. I had time to spend with my family and friends. My life was fine with me in my small world.

Six months or so went by after the convention, and I was called into the boss's office. He said, "Sit down; I need to talk to you. Nadine, I have to let you go."

I said, "What is wrong with my work?"

He said, "It's not your work. My wife is not comfortable with a divorced woman working for me."

This was a man who, even if he were a millionaire, I would not have given any time after hours even if I were starving—and I was struggling to have food on the table at the time.

I needed that job badly, and he knew I was supporting myself and a child and that there were not many jobs available. His wife was a very pretty woman. I thought about how insecure she must be.

He then had the nerve to say, "I will help you find another job."

I said, "Do not worry. I was looking for one when I came here. I can fend for myself." I had a lot of pride and wanted him know I could stand on my own.

What would you tell someone about me if you were recommending me for a job? I thought. *Certainly your wife doesn't trust you.* If something like that happened to anyone else today, it would mean a lawsuit for sure, although I wouldn't sue now, just as I did not sue then.

I saw my first discrimination in New York. It was at a big restaurant at Forty-Second and Lexington for a Thanksgiving holiday lunch in the '50s. About two hundred people and a handsome, beautifully dressed black man walked in with an equally beautiful blonde. I will never forget that sight. The room got very quiet as they were led all the way to the last table by the kitchen.

I wanted to stand up and cheer. They walked as if they owned the place. I was so proud of them and ashamed of the people who acted as if they were better.

I have always wondered if they were actors with the ease they handled the situation. We lived across from the El Morocco. Tom gambled a lot and placed his bets with the newspaper stand guy on corner of Fifty-Second and Second. Sometimes he sent me. I would take a little money from his pockets at night and make a call to Inez, who lived in Jackson Heights in Queens, New York. Defying was a real no-no, and he sure did not like my sister, as he felt her dislike.

I ran many times but always ended up going back.

I called Inez as often as possible but could not talk long; just hearing her voice was what I needed.

CHAPTER 4

The Same Old Fear

When I had just lost my job at Arkansas Medical, Tom came back with his threats as always. Despite being divorced, I went back to him due to fear and the pressures I was dealing with.

He brought us to New York, which to me was so different from anyplace I had lived. Time went on, and it was not any better with him than it had ever been.

Because I never told my family much that was going on, he somehow would find where I was. This, needless to say, freaked me out. He started telling how he would take the baby from me, and I knew he could easily grab her and run. I was with him again in that awful fear.

He had become more cunning. He said he would drive by my parents' house and tell me how he saw my dad walking with his cane by himself and how easy it would be to just hit and run. Talk about wanting to leave Arkansas as fast as I could. I did.

Inez lived in Jackson Heights, New York. I saw very little of her, and I know she seethed when we went out to her house. Though Tom would always try to seem so nice around her, she knew better.

One would have to wonder how we always lived in a nice apartment in the best neighborhoods. He carried a briefcase that was always locked, and he always had it in his possession. I would now guess that he was either into very heavy gambling or drugs. I still do not know.

I know he had cash and wore very expensive suits—I am talking $2,000–$3,000 suits back in those days. He bought my clothes, and they were always very sexy. They were always good. I hated it. It was just more control he had over me.

He did not drink, but he did use sleeping pills, and he always was going to different doctors to get them. When I look back, I probably could have sneaked a few pills into something, but of course, I would have never done that.

I would never remarry him, but he did not care; he was in control.

I now know that fear and embarrassment are big factors that allow such control. I was isolated from family and friends and had no contact with the world without his sanction. Tom listened to every phone call to or from Inez. If I didn't say to her what Tom wanted me to, all hell would break loose.

Do not ever say to a woman, "Well, why don't you just leave?" Help them to leave, because they cannot do it alone. It becomes impossible to do so.

One of the worst episodes with him was one night when I was sound asleep and I awoke as he had hold of both my feet while standing at the end of the bed. He pulled me off the bed, and of course, I landed on my back. There was no warning and no explanation of why he would do this. Much damage was done, and early the next morning, I went to Dr. Keggi. I could hardly walk and was in great pain. He examined me and asked what happened. Embarrassed, I lied and said that I fell off a ladder. He looked me in the eye and said, "No, that is not what happened."

He later knew my life had changed when I went to him after marrying Bud Schramm. He never asked a question about Tom. Then later, he met Bud. Abusers, I now know, are always cowards and always very unstable. That makes them hard to deal with, as their personalities change within minutes. They are also sociopaths who dominate and have no feelings for other human beings.

Tom used his fist on me often and even a couple of times put his hands around my throat, choking me until I almost passed out. After every time he beat me, he would tell me he loved me and that he was sorry and that he would never do it again.

Did I ever say I loved him? No, never once in all the time I was with him. He could take my body, but he could not take my heart or soul.

Even looking in the mirror, I would say, "Never give up in your own mind who you really are." Needless to say, I wavered many times, but the memories of my childhood life stayed though it all. I knew I was loved by all my family and friends, but they must have thought I was crazy. I was a mystery. I was so erratic, and I never had been in growing up. I ran away so many times with my daughter. More than once, I went to the port authority bus station and took a bus just to wherever they were going—not too far, as I always had very little money. No matter how hard I tried, he always found me.

Of course, I would call my family, but they had no idea of much of the stuff that was the happening to me. I needed that connection so badly; it was the only stability in my life. Even knowing I had a loving family, I still could not tell them how bad it was.

He called my sister Annette often when I ran. She always told him flat out, "If I knew where she was, I would not tell you." She detested him and had watched the change in me.

I would be in a town where I knew no one, thinking I could hide, looking for work with no recommendation and with a baby. Would you hire that person? No one did.

It was always back to the same scene.

Today, I fear almost nothing. If anyone tried to hurt me or anyone around me, he or she would probably be the one who needed to run. But the funny thing is that bullies know how to pick victims. My innocence played a great part in my not being able to handle what was happening. Having never seen such behavior as his, I was ill equipped to handle him.

I left Tom and brought Mary to Little Rock with me. I got a job with three neurosurgeons in Little Rock. Three other women worked there, and they were very nice to me. The doctors were also very easy to work for, and I enjoyed working there. They, of course, had patients with very difficult issues. My sister-in-law Nita took care of Mary, and we lived with them for a while. Then I got a tiny little house for the two of us.

I was working for this group of doctors when Tom called to say his mother was dying, and she was begging to see her granddaughter. I said that would happen only if he signed papers by a lawyer. He said, "She only has hours to live, and she is begging to see Mary." He said he would return her to me in just a few days. His mother was a lovely woman who he treated badly. She did love her only grandchild. What could I do? Deny a grandmother seeing her only grandchild at what I thought would be one last time? He did not return her, so I went to get her.

His mother was not even sick; it was just another of his many lies. Why did I believe him? I should have known by then, but who could tell such a lie about his own mother?

I had to figure out a way to get Mary back.

I drove to Irving, Texas, to get her. Of course, I did not have any luck with that. I stayed. Then his sister started trying to get me to have him committed. I said, "You know I am not going to be able to do that. How come, in all the years, no one in this family has done it?"

Of course, they were as troubled as I was; he had had great anger in his early years. I did not blame them, either; it seemed insurmountable.

I found out later that he had married a young lady from Houston, Texas, before he had married me. Of course, he did not tell me, but his sister Anne did. That young lady divorced him and then married a police officer very quickly. I am sure I know why.

In the 1960s, I got a job at Hoffman-La Roche, a pharmaceutical company in Dallas, and it turned out to be one I really enjoyed. We lived in Irving, which was a half hour or so away. I loved it, and I was away from Tom all day.

Mary was in school and was picked up by his sister Jayne, who was a lovely person and who did much for me. I ran to their house many times. I even stayed sometimes and would go to work in her clothes even though they did not fit me well.

Tom came home to our apartment with a monkey in a huge cage at about 3:00 a.m. He woke me to help him carry it in. The cage was big and ugly. Where to sit it? In the living room, of course.

He hung out in a girlie joint in Dallas that was owned by Jack Ruby, and he had made his purchase at that bar. Jack said he met a circus man who wanted to sell the monkey. It had all kind of clothes. He was told he had a monkey who could do tricks. Well, that was some smart monkey, and Tom bought it. It never let Tom put clothes on it. He may have performed tricks for the other man, but all he did was masturbate very often. That was not what I needed to happen in front of my child. Every time he tried to touch the monkey, it screeched and bit him. I loved seeing that—fitting the justice ... and by a monkey.

Tom went out and bought heavy gloves. Let me tell you that monkey drove him crazy; it always went to the top of the drapes and would not come down. He called me several times to come home from work. I just said I could not or I would be fired. I tried to give it away, but no one of course wanted it. It was just as well; I would have felt guilty. And then one day the monkey was just no longer there.

Tom's family members were very nice and treated me well. They knew how bad he was, as he treated his mother and his other sister terribly. They all stayed clear of him as much as possible, especially Jayne's husband, Jay, who was a wonderful man who put up with a lot. None of them wanted to deal with him, and they did not know what to do with him. It was very reasonable thinking.

I worked the earliest computers called keypunch. I was so fast that the manager, Joe, used to laugh and say they needed faster machines for me.

I worked there when JFK was killed. That morning, Joe had made a remark while we were having coffee that he should not be coming to Dallas and he would be lucky if he got out alive.

There was ill feeling with a lot of people with some of his thinking on race. Many of us thought and felt as JFK did and that it was way past time for major change.

At break time, Joe came in and just kept saying, "I did not mean for him to be hurt." We did not know at that time Kennedy had been shot, but this man had been listening to the radio and heard it. The airport was only a mile from our place, and we had watched the plane come in for landing.

What they did not tell the people was that he was dead on arrival at the hospital. They also told people a total lie about where the shots came from that killed him. You have to know the terrain, and it was not right for the shots to come from the depository where Oswald was.

We were all dazed, and when it came time to leave at 5:00 p.m., we thought he would live. I drove the thruway home at five or ten miles an hour; it was usually bumper to bumper at seventy-five to eighty miles an hour on the expressway between Dallas and Fort Worth. It was like slow motion.

Irving was country then. I lived just down from where Bush Stadium was later built and where big money was made by pushing out small farmers for very little money. Farmers could not fight the power of the developers. They covered up everything that happened. They told what they wanted people to hear.

I thought Lee Oswald no doubt was a loose cannon but not, in my opinion, the one who shot JFK. I did not believe Jack Ruby had much of anything to do with JFK's death, either. He was a small-time club owner who was running a pimp joint, and a name was needed. Nothing fit the picture to me as it was told by the Warren Commission. Who was responsible? We will never know.

Also I thought perhaps it was the Mafia, who disliked JFK and Bobby because of their trysts with their girlfriends. Well, those were my thoughts only, not an accusation. But I always am willing to put money on my feelings, and I would place a good bet on this. One could not believe the way they were saying it happened. First, the terrain was not right for Oswald to be where they said and for the bullet to have come from the depository. JFK was no doubt dead when he arrived at the hospital. The driver of the bus Oswald got on died very shortly after. I do not remember his age, but he was young.

There were about seven deaths in all of the people who were there. One that I remember vividly was one man from Texas who was at the scene. He was walking on the boardwalk in Florida, and suddenly, a plate-glass window blew out and killed him. Newspapers wanted no part of writing about any of them, it seemed. There was much control on what was printed.

CHAPTER 5

Changes to a Better Life

Shortly after that, things were not good, as usual, but I made a trip with Tom to New York. Before that trip, I had found some small samples of perfumes in a place where they made concrete garden figures. They were very good copies of name-brand perfumes. This is how I got the idea for my first business. In hindsight, I feel it was almost a God-given idea. I had never had a business, and at the time, it was very unusual for a woman to own a business. I asked the owner in Texas, Tom Taylor, what he was doing with the perfumes, and he said that he was just selling them. I asked if I could use them to see what I could do with them. He said, "You can do anything you want; I am just selling them."

I wanted to put the perfumes in beautiful bottles and package them in boxes with company logos for them give to their customers. I have no idea how I came up with this idea, but I was the first to do giveaways with company logos. I copied the name of the man who had shipped them. It was a man named Healey from Long Island City, New York. I called him and asked for an appointment. When we took the trip to New York, I left Mary Anne with Jayne.

It was a very long trip, and just outside Cincinnati, Ohio, it was getting dusk when Tom pulled over on a main interstate highway and said, "Get out." He took my handbag.

I did not have much but my driver's license and very little money. He opened the door and shoved me out. As usual, his tantrum came out of the blue with no warning whatsoever. I stood on the side of the road petrified for a long time, cars whizzing by me. About a half hour later, he pulled up and said, "Get in." Of course I did; I had no choice.

We stayed at the Eastgate Hotel in New Jersey just outside the Lincoln Tunnel. He had one of his fits for no reason and really did a number on me. I had become quite good at covering up black eyes and wearing clothes to cover damage.

When I went downstairs to get breakfast, the owner of the hotel, Harry Birns, came and sat next to me. He introduced himself and said, "My maids tell me you are in trouble. If you want to get away from him, you will be protected. You can have a free room and food. The maids will retrieve your clothes or whatever is yours and bring it to your new room when he goes looking for you."

I said, "Thank you, and I will take you up on it." I felt I'd been touched by an angel.

I went to the new room.

Tom went looking for me. He came back to discover my things missing. All I had with me were summer clothes, and it was the beginning of fall.

I had one small suitcase and a few dollars. I knew at that point it had to be the end. I knew I had to end this madness for Mary and me permanently. The only way was to totally disappear from him. I knew Jayne and her husband would take care of Mary until I could reach out for her when I had myself settled. I never thought he would take responsibility of keeping her, and I had full custody through the divorce.

I got in touch with Jayne. She told me he had left immediately with Mary, and she did not know where he was. His mother, who really cared for me, would not tell me where he had gone if she knew. I understood her, as he treated her so poorly, and she also was afraid of him. I certainly understood all their reluctance. Mary had every right to think that I had abandoned her. He, I am sure, told her that. I never thought he would take her, as he had never taken responsibility for anything. No doubt he thought I would come back because of her. She had to be scared and alone as a child if I was afraid as an adult.

I had Inez in New York, but I did not tell any of my family where I was. He always found me—I will never know how. This time, I had to be absolutely sure. I would leave no trails. I did not contact anyone other than the one call to his sister until three months later. I called the one person I knew he would not call—Henry Clay, a lawyer. Tom probably did not even know him even though we had been neighbors a few years before on East Fifty-Fourth Street in New York City.

Thank goodness he remembered me. He said, "Are you still with that jerk?"

I said, "That's the reason I am calling you." I knew I would need help, and he was the only one I could think of. I was not even sure he would remember me. I was on the very edge of a complete nervous breakdown. I could not hold a cup of coffee with one hand because I shook so.

Henry sent a lawyer from his office to pick me up from the hotel in New Jersey to bring me to his office. He said, "Do not worry; he carries a licensed gun, and he is big. You will be protected."

When we got to Henry's office, he asked me to tell all that was going on, and I told him.

Henry said, "Nadine, I have an apartment you can have."

I said, "Henry, I have very little money. How much is it?"

He said, "It is very small."

"How much?"

"It is seventy-five dollars a month."

Now I knew that was probably not what he got, and I protested, but not too much. It was no bigger than my kitchen today, but it had a New York kitchen and bathroom. It became my palace. I did not have to worry about being abused.

I had only one thing on my mind: get my daughter from Tom.

I had the need and desire to make something of myself. I was under great stress, but I knew it was the last time I would go back no matter what happened, because my life had become such a nightmare. Mary Anne was old enough to now know how things were, at least in a child's mind. I knew if I did not take hold, I probably would not survive to be there when and if I got my daughter back.

I was very lucky that I had a friend who really cared about what was happening to me. Henry asked me what I intended to do. I told him that my plan was to get a job and get my life back together.

He asked me why we had come to New York, and I told him about the perfume, and he said it sounded like a good idea and that I should go with those plans.

I told him, "I have no money and need to just get my feet on the ground to pay for rent and food and get my daughter."

He said, "Listen, I have some cash lying around, and I want to give you money to go ahead with it."

I said, "I can't take the chance of not being able to pay back."

He said, "You will never fail; I believe in you."

To have someone say that to me was so beautiful, and I was very touched.

He put the money in my hands the next day. He had asked how much it would take. Finally, I said $1,500, and he said that no business could start with that small amount, so he gave me $3,000.

He said, "That is really not enough to start a business, and I have more when you need it."

I started immediately to put it together by getting a box maker and bottles and talking to the chemist in Long Island City, New York.

The chemist had worked for Revlon and had developed many of its name-brand perfumes. He had concocted copies of every well-known perfume. Actually, they were the same; he just had to call them copies so as not to infringe.

I got prices, and they were very cheap. He and his wife worked out of their garage in Long Island City, New York. What a sight, and they were very nice people—salt of the earth. I loved working with them, and they loved my ideas.

How my luck had changed with the help of so many wonderful people. I looked up box makers and found one on Spring Street who said he could do it all for me—making the boxes and putting the print on—and he gave me prices that I felt I could afford for the project. I had sample boxes made up with sample company logos. Next, I had to find the perfect bottles. On Fifth Avenue, I found a supplier and picked small, beautiful bottles that would fit the boxes I had designed. Then I got my first few quarts of the most popular copies—Joy, Chanel, Shalimar, White Shoulders, and some of the other popular ones.

Now I realized that I had no clothes to make sales calls to top executives. I saw a resale shop called Michael's Resale. It was upstairs, and up I went, and I could not believe the beautiful suits and dresses. All were very cheap, and I bought a couple of dresses and a winter coat for less than one hundred dollars. I shopped there for years and still stop by sometimes just as a reminder of how my life has changed.

The next agenda item was one of the most important parts: making calls for appointments. I would call and find out the names of the highest-up in a company, hang up, and then call later to speak to that person. I could not afford to waste any time with underlings who could not make the decision to buy. There were few women in business at that point, but I think I got many appointments simply because a man could not believe some woman saying she had something they really needed—especially saying, "I have something you will want; just give me two minutes."

I sold because I was one of the first to do promotions as giveaways, especially with perfumes in beautiful boxes with their logos. I was young and fairly attractive, so every day if I made four business calls, I got at least one call at the end of the day about going to dinner. Needless to say, I had no interest, and I knew most of them were married and just cheaters. My mind was totally focused on selling. I paid Henry back in three months. Oh, what a relief. When I gave him the money, I said, "I owe you interest, but I do not know how to figure it. You are the lawyer, so tell me."

He said, "Nadine, there is no interest on the money, but sometime in your life, you will do the same as I did for someone else."

I have done it several times and have always been paid back. The rule is still the same as was given to me.

I worked twenty hours many days between selling, designing the boxes, filling the bottles from quart bottles, delivering, billing, and all the other things. I got so tired of saying no to dinners that I came up with a line that I used. Most top executives back then were in their fifties or older and married. So my reply to their invitation was "Oh, another married man looking for a night out?"

There was usually a moment of silence, and then, being embarrassed, many said, "Oh, I wanted to talk to you about an order."

I would say, "How about me coming in to see you tomorrow morning around ten or eleven o'clock?"

I got several orders that way. Shame on me, but hey, I needed orders to survive.

It's funny, though—it's the way I met my fabulous second husband. I went to take a second order from a fine gentleman, Mr. Ralph Endler, who worked at Railway Express—similar to the UPS of today. He was a man who had not asked me out to dinner and had given me my biggest orders. He had bought and loved the product, so I went to his office, and when the secretary took me in, another gentleman was there. *Handsome and such a nice man*, I thought. *Some woman sure is lucky to have him as a husband.*

Well, that afternoon, sure enough, he called me. I gave him the same line. *Gee, nice, but a cheater too*, I thought. There was the long silence, and he said, "Pardon me?"

I repeated it, and he answered, "Well, I am separated."

I said, "Oh, for tonight?"

He said, "Well, I have been out of the house for three months and filed for divorce."

I said, "Well, in that case, I will go."

I remembered what I had thought that morning. I was not wrong. He was everything I thought he would be or even better.

I did not think I would ever meet a man I would trust again. I tried to make him mad, and he would look at me funny and just laugh. I finally said, "I just wanted to see if you would hit me."

He looked horrified and said, "I could never hit a woman. I never even liked to fight when I was a kid."

We had dinner every night, and eventually I told him that I had something to talk with him about. He smiled and asked, "What?"

I told him I had a bad marriage and that I never intended to be seriously involved and that I did not want to waste his time. Once was enough for me.

He just smiled and asked if we could continue on the basis we were. It took a year to get a divorce in New Jersey, and we had such a good relationship of conversation and sharing food and music, and that for him was enough.

He had his daughters, Valerie and Vicki, every weekend, and he introduced me quickly. He always invited me to be with them, and I tried to get him just to spend his weekends with them, but he said, "No, they always ask for you."

I think it must have been so hard for him to know what to do with them, as they now loved clothes, and what man loves to shop for children's clothing? I would take them shopping and always bought for them.

They were the same age as Mary, so needless to say, I looked at them and thought of how Mary must be growing.

Inez loved Bud from the day she met him. She constantly asked me after six months if we were talking seriously, and I would answer, "Of course—we laugh, and then we talk about the serious things in the world or of the people around us."

She would say, "No, I mean about your relationship."

I would say, "I do not know what you mean."

She would say, "Marriage."

I always told her, "You know I never intend to get married again; I have told everyone who knows me that. I am capable of making a living for myself, and I have the problem of finding Mary. That is foremost in my life."

She prodded me the whole three years. My answer was always the same.

She finally said to me, "Well, someday a woman is going to meet him, and she will know what a person he is and take him away."

I laughed and said, "Then I guess it is not love."

Bud had told me of his family and how they had become truckers. They became the biggest Allied agents. Bud's father was even president of the company. He wanted me to know his background and about his family. He had been very close with his father, and in talking to him, I knew they had a strong bond.

Louis Schramm Sr., Bud's grandfather, boarded a steamer at the age of sixteen to the docks of New York in the late 1800s from Germany. He came alone and worked and saved enough money to buy a horse and wagon in the late 1800s. He moved coal in the Chelsea district of New York City. The coal was used in coal furnaces in an area that was mostly inhabited by tenement dwellers. He also moved people and their furniture in the same wagon as the coal.

He got many requests to move people to Pennsylvania and elsewhere out of New York City. He could not make any money just going there and coming back empty-handed, so he met with movers there and set up a system to work to each other's advantage, getting a return load from them. Then when they came to New York, he would arrange a move back for them. He got more horses and wagons as the need arose. When motor cars came, he upgraded. He was then one of the original founders of Allied Van Lines—those big orange trailers you see on the roads today.

That is the premise that Allied still uses today by arranging shipments out for all agents from their main office in Illinois.

His sons, Louis Jr., Frederick, and Ray, all stayed in the business. Frederick also died young, leaving a wife and four young children.

I think every Allied agent who came to New York called Bud. He was the youngest board member at that time. They knew he would see that they got to the best restaurants and the best shows and also have time with him. I met many of them, and they were all fun people. They all had one problem, and that was to constantly talk about his father.

Louis Jr., Bud and Bob's father, was president of Allied for about ten years and was a great a leader. He was revered by all. He was known for his commanding speeches and leadership. If a thousand people came to an Allied convention, a thousand were in the room when he spoke. I never had the pleasure meeting him, as he died very young at fifty-seven, before I met Bud.

I was very busy, as I was selling to banks, hotels, and all kinds of organizations. I met many interesting people, and one of the fun ones was Saul Richman, who was called Mr. Broadway. He was a publicity agent who had many theaters as clients. He also represented many prizefighters and show business personalities. He took me to Sardi's. Oh, did I feel grand going there. He would point out stars from Broadway shows. Sardi's was and is still today a very popular venue for before- and after-theater dinner.

Saul would call and ask me if I wanted to see a top show. I loved that. He usually put a folding chair for me in the front row of any show that was sold out. I would say, "Saul, you can't do that." He just laughed.

Then he called me and wanted me to do a men's cologne as a giveaway for a billiard tournament. To my surprise, the two who were to be a main event were Minnesota Fats and Peter Falk. I designed a green box with crossed black cue sticks, and I called it Mr. Cue. Lo and behold, I got a call from a Colgate Palmolive lawyer saying they wanted to buy six bottles. I told them it was not for sale a few at a time; it was only to be bought and given free, and it must have advertising on it.

They were persistent. I figured out what they were

thinking. I said, "Send a messenger; I will give him six bottles." They did send the messenger. I soon got a letter saying that I was infringing on their product name.

I said, "And how is that? I don't see any connection with cue sticks crossed on a box and a toothpaste called Cue."

If they were smart, they would have asked to buy the label. Instead they said, "Well, we will take it to court."

I said, "Fine, then, I will win, and you will pay me." I never heard from them again. I loved making them back down. I was a little farm girl from Arkansas who would no longer be pushed around.

I had dated Bud for maybe three months when I met his mother, Denise, for the first time on a business trip to Florida. I told Bud I had to go down to around Fort Lauderdale on business. He said, "Well, maybe I will go and visit my mother if it is okay with you."

She was in Golden Beach, and I was going to be staying in a hotel closer to Miami. He wanted me to have dinner with the two of them, which I agreed to, only for him to call me, saying he wanted to talk to me. I said, "I will be at the pool."

He arrived, and I could tell he was upset. He had come to tell me that his mother refused to join us. She considered him still married until the divorce was final. I said, "You go have dinner with her; I will see you in New York."

Well, he did have dinner with her. His mother was such a total lady and from the old school. Since there was never a divorce in the family, she was torn apart having to tell family and friends. It was very embarrassing to her. His wife had moved out as Bud was coming back from a board meeting of Allied Van Lines. Bud told me it was the best thing that ever happened to him, as they were married young, and he admitted he did not know real love until he met me. He said he did not even know he had a bad marriage; he just thought that's the way it was.

Bud was now in a delicate situation—having to handle his mother, whom he loved dearly, and a woman whom he now wanted to introduce her to. He called the next morning to talk to me. He had told her, "I am having dinner with Nadine tonight; you can join us if you want."

She said, "Well, why not have her come here for a drink, and then we will all go to dinner." So I said okay, and he picked me up. I was not sure that was such a good idea, as I already knew she did not approve of our relationship. I did not feel the need to meet his mother, and I said so.

He said, "No, she is going to have to deal with us, as I intend to spend most of my time with you. I have always shared my weekends with her since my father's death. I am still willing to do that, but only if she accepts you—and she will if she takes the time to know you."

So I went.

I walked into a beautiful home, and she was such a lovely, petite lady—a true Auntie Mame. She asked Bud to help make the drinks. He told me the next day that when they went into the bar area, she said to him, "Bud, she's a lovely young lady and smart."

Bud replied, "What did you expect I would bring to introduce to you?"

I rarely get nervous, but I was that night. I spilled my drink.

I waved my hand as I was talking. All I could think was that it was a disaster. I imagined she thought I had done it on purpose.

I think it was the first drink I ever dropped—and the last one. I dropped a screwdriver—orange juice and vodka—on her thick white carpet, and yet she treated it as if it were a wooden floor. She was so gracious. We laughed and had such a good time. From then on, she and I were best friends. She loved to party, and that fit my style as well as Bud's.

When she came back to New York a month later, she immediately invited me to her home on North Haven, just over the bridge from Sag Harbor, an old whaling town that is very nostalgic. It is still very beautiful, and I was fortunate to know it in the days when it was still the old families who had been there for many years.

Bud's mother was widowed very young, and Bud had always made sure he shared his time with her. Most of the time if we traveled, she was with us. She was the perfect mother-in-law.

Bud and his mother laughed many times about a thing that had happened when she and Bud's father had bought their house on North Haven. His two brothers also bought, and for many years, they were just known as the Schramm brothers. There were one hundred acres of land on North Haven, and the brothers were offered a chance to buy. Two of the brothers—one being Bud's father—offered $30,000 and thought for sure he had it, only for someone to offer $35,000 and get it. Well, that property could never be built on for many years.

They of course knew it would someday build up, and today, there are many huge homes there. Well, taxes had to be paid about forty years before developing because of all the permits, so I do not think it was such a good deal; they probably did not have that kind of money to pay taxes with no returns for so long.

He spent his time there every weekend from a very young age, living and schooling in Westchester. At a young age, he was working in the city at the family business, Chelsea Warehouses. They were cofounders of Allied Van Lines along with the Morgan family. (I recently have seen a moving company with the name Chelsea Moving, but it is not ours; it is a new company.) Then he spent weekends on the water that he loved. He had a small motorboat, and he spent as much time as possible fishing and just being away from the pressing issues of business. He never seemed spoiled by that childhood. I do know he missed his father, with him being away so much of the time when Bud was little. As soon as Bud was old enough, his father took him along. No doubt Bud was his favorite.

With Denise and I, there was one disagreement, and it was so funny. She was a good cook but did not enjoy it, so Bud and I always cooked on weekends. We always had a few in the kitchen as we made dinners, most times the three of us. I was rinsing greens for the salad. Denise walked over and looked at what I was doing and said, "Nadine, that's not the way I do it."

I burst out laughing and said, "Did you ever think you may have done it wrong all your life?"

She and Bud both laughed with me. End of salad lessons.

I was privileged to hear many stories from my mother-in-law about the days of bootlegging. The 21 Club was a speakeasy, and the Schramms were very involved in what went on in New York.

Bud's father, Louis Schramm Jr., was a friend of the

colorful Mayor Jimmy Walker. They spent time at the 21 Club. I had the pleasure of being shown the basement wine cellar and felt strong nostalgia thinking they had probably been in that room with all the intrigue of doing a little drinking or maybe a lot from the fun stories I heard about them from Denise. It had an entrance from the rear of the building to hide from the law during Prohibition.

Then there was an old-style speakeasy named Bill's Gay Nineties on East Fifty-Fourth Street. The partners eventually divided the business, but they both have survived. It was later changed to just Bill's. Bud and I went there after hockey games. I go there regularly now to dance and have fun with lots of people who go for the same reason. You walk into a place and go back to the feeling of yesteryear. At least I do.

It was a piano bar. People sang, danced, and had fun. Some of the voices were great, others were terrible, but everyone was having a great time. They still have the old door in the back that the wall turns to let the people in that was used during Prohibition. It has old original photographs of fighters, race horses, and so on during Prohibition. This original Bill's closed, and now you have new owners. Bud knew a man, Jack Fitzpatrick, who was an executive at the new Madison Square Garden. There was a bar across from the Garden where all the hockey players went after the games.

We went to all the games. The owner would let people come in and drink during the game, but when he knew the game had ended, he would always say, "We are closing in about forty-five minutes." Everyone but just maybe four of us had to leave. We could be there when the teams came in.

We got to meet them all not just once but many times. Those guys could drink ten beers so fast. They were all dehydrated after the game—Rod Gilbert, who at the time was a young rising star for the Rangers, Phil Esposito, and many others, but mostly it was the out-of-town players. It was so exciting, and all of them were young. The New York Rangers were mostly going home. Most were Canadians, as it was their sport. I think at that time there was only one American player.

One night, Phil Esposito was sitting next to me, and we were talking. He started running his finger over the bar in the beer and ashes, so I said, "Phil, what are you doing?"

He said, "Looking for my contact lens."

I told him, "You cannot put it back in even if you find it."

At about that time, he found it popped it back in. He said, "Don't worry; I drink enough to kill any germs."

It was funny to see them play and hit so hard and then drink together in the old Madison Square Garden on Eighth Avenue and Fiftieth. We went to games twice a week back when there were only six teams. Bud's father had taken him as a young boy, and they had reserved seats. I loved it from the beginning. It was so fast, and I loved learning the plays and then guessing what plays they were going to do. It was another thing we could share that was new to me. He had told me a lot, and I could tell it was his sport.

We of course had beer and popcorn. Then the game started, and boy, it was rougher than anything I had ever seen. First of all, growing up in Arkansas, I never saw much ice on the ground, much less on a rink, and I was impressed with them being able to move like they were flying, never falling down. Everyone was yelling, "Kill 'em!"

I said to Bud, "Boy, this is really a rough sport!" I started to get into the game, but then there is a huge fight. The New York Rangers and the other team were coming up into the crowd over the boards close to us. Skates were sticking up in the air, and it was just below us. I said to Bud, "Listen, I think this is going to turn into a riot. Is this normal? I think we should try to get out of here."

He said, "No, it will be all right. The referees will handle it."

They did, but it took more time than I wanted. Bud told me later that he also was worried. He had never seen anything like it before. Sure enough, it was all over the papers the next day.

That is when they put up plexiglass around whole rink instead of just around the end behind the goalie, which was to just catch pucks that did not go in. That night went down in hockey history, and it was my first game. Things seem to always happen on my watch. Thank goodness most of the time they are funny.

CHAPTER 6

A Very Complicated Time

I had no news all this time about Mary, but my mind was always on her, wondering what was happening to her. I knew it was not good, and I felt I had let her down terribly. I tried not to talk about it all the time to Bud. He was always a good listener, but he could really give no advice. He always said that the table was round, and it would turn. It was a nightmare that would not go away. Bud was so good. This hurt more than any fist or any black eye. He would let me talk and then say, "Someday, she will find you." But I knew she would be scarred forever with his teaching. I knew he had turned her against me.

At this time, I started to think of when it had begun. Tom twisted her mind in ways at the time that seemed just to be his pattern of control. When she was very young, she started saying she wanted to take her bath alone and then choose her clothes. As little as she was, she wanted to dress herself. I realized too late that he was teaching her to pull away from me. He made a game of holding me down and telling her to hit me. He made it look like a game to her. It was not. How degrading it was.

She was actually a very good child. I never had to spank her, and the only time I had a problem was when I had taken her to the dime store to get something I needed. She wanted something, and I said no; I did not have the money to pay for it. She lay down in middle of the aisle and started crying and screaming. I picked her up, carried her outside to the sidewalk, and said to her, "Do not ever do that again. If I can, I will buy for you; if I cannot, there is a reason. If you do it again, I will not take you shopping another time with me." It was the same way my father had been so effective with me. It worked.

During the years when I did not know where she was, I did not sleep much. When I did, it would end up with bad dreams. I kept busy. Business was good. When I was not working, I was always with Bud. Bud and I did everything together. I was back to spending lots of time with Inez. She loved going out with us. She was never was as adventurous as I was, but she did get a big kick out of being included in so many things. Bud was never upset with me including her, as he was always including his friends. All melded into a happy group.

Inez had lots of friends, but all were married. She loved

to talk about what was going on with all our family scattered all over the country. I loved it too. I was back in the family loop. She loved cooking, and she made great Italian meals, especially her tomato sauce, which she learned from her ex-mother-in-law. She also had learned recipes from restaurants. The Italian was the best, though, with all the seasonings and cheeses.

Time flew by, and I kept so busy with my business. It was me still doing it all. It was like my baby. I was meeting people and learning a lot about the business world. I felt as if I were proving to myself that I was efficient as I had been as a young person back on that farm. I was making money and saving much of it. Henry Clay would never take more money for his little studio. I had expanded quickly and was using his basement in the apartment building as my perfume workshop. I filled the bottles and packaged them there while Henry did his woodworking, which was his hobby.

Henry was quite the character. What he had not told me with all my problems was that he was going through a divorce and had young children. It was a painful time, I am sure. He was so funny when I started dating Bud, and I had introduced them. Henry remarked, "He is a nice chap." A few days later, he came to me and said, "I checked this Bud Schramm guy out, and he is the real thing."

Well, I had done my homework too—no hidden surprises for me on this one. Bud was an attractive man, and being divorced, he was a target for many women. I did not worry about it. However, a couple of times, it was thrown in my face. There were two sisters who lived in his neighborhood, and one was determined to try for him. She came to Johnny's Bar on East Forty-Seventh Street all the time, and we were regulars.

One night, we came from a hockey game with Jack and Hilda Kirkeby. In she came, and she stood in between Bud and me as she always did. For a year, she would only refer to me as Bud's friend.

Jack and Hilda knew the scene that night. I was having a good time. I had no real jealousy, but I was tired of her. I had a drink in my hand, and I let it slide out of hand. I had a direct hit to her feet. I, of course, was very apologetic and helped wipe off her shoes. She had on a new glitzy pair. She was so upset and said, "Oh, my new shoes!" She left, going to the chauffeured car that she always came in. She was a nurse to a rich elderly woman from Sutton Place. She must have put her to bed with a sleeping pill early most nights and gone out on the town. No one suspected that I did it on purpose, but I told them. Everyone thought it was funny, including the owner, so we had a good laugh.

Another time, a group of models had come in to town

from Norfolk, Virginia, for a weekend, and they called Bud. He was having a party in his apartment with his mother, uncle, and aunt, along with some friends. He put the phone down and came to me to tell me who was on the line and that he had told them he was having a party. He asked me what to do. "Should I have them come over or what?"

I said, "If you want, invite them." Now I am not that dumb. He must have been out with one of them, so I wanted to see the competition. Well, one was more beautiful than the other. We decided to all go dancing around Sixtieth Street and Fifth Avenue, where there was great music.

Bud and I were dancing, and he asked me if he should dance with them. "Of course," I said. "They are your guests." Bud was now sweating it out. I was laughing. *Typical man*, I thought. *He got in a mess and doesn't know how to handle it.* They were models who came to New York doing shoots for JCPenney catalogs.

Well, Budd did have good taste.

After his dance, some of the other men started dancing with them. The wives were not so happy. One who was most unhappy was the aunt. She wore her hair in braids in a wrap around her head. She sat at the table, let her hair down, and said, "When I put my hair down, it means I am mad." When Uncle Ray came back to the table, they left. It must have been the hair. He had no doubt seen it come down before. The party broke up shortly after.

Another time, Bud called me and said an agent had come into town—not saying whether it was a man or a woman—and he was going to have a business dinner. I said fine. Then he asked, "What are you going to do?"

I said, "Do not worry; I will be busy."

As it happened, a few minutes later, a fellow who was an executive of JCPenney that I had gone out with a few times called and asked me to dinner. I said yes. What is good for the goose is good for the gander.

It turned out to be a very interesting evening for me and my escort. We went to Le Pavillon at Fifty-Seventh and Park Avenue and were seated next to Jackie Kennedy and Bobby Kennedy.

Needless to say, we were very pleased to be in such company.

She was definitely one of the most beautiful women I have ever seen. There was one thing, though, that you could not help but notice: she had the smallest legs I have ever seen on a grown woman, and her feet were very long and thin—maybe a size ten. When you looked at that face, you were taken aback with it. Believe me, she was striking. It kept our attention for a long time. We had several glasses of wine, and they drank wine and champagne, I remember.

What was so interesting was I felt they were like daters, not kin. I always say women pick up on the looks and the eye contact when there is something going on. This was sometime after JFK's death. I could not wait to tell Henry Clay, and I did the next day. He said, "No way—just a good brother-in-law." I laughed.

Two weeks later, Henry called me and said, "You were right."

I said, "About what?"

He said, "Jackie and Bobby." He had been to Stratton for skiing, and they were there for the weekend. There was now no doubt in his mind, either, and Henry was a player.

I thought this dinner Bud was having was not with an agent, because he always included me with his out-of-town agents. After two more days, the so-called agent had not left town. These were about the only nights we had not been together since we met. I thought, well, maybe it was a buddy of his, and they wanted to talk of things alone, which I thought nothing of.

He almost always asked me to meet him at his apartment. He had a little patio, so we went out with a drink. There was one problem, though: we had to go through his bedroom to get there.

Going through, I saw a shoe sticking out from under his bed. It was not mine, but I picked it up and said, "Oh, someone left a shoe." He was mortified. I just went on out with my drink and never said another word about the shoe, and he did not, either. What could he say?

Three days later, I got a call. He wanted to come in midmorning to see me. *What is going on?* I wondered. Maybe he met someone else—the owner of that shoe, maybe.

He walked in and was a wreck. He said, "I have something I want you to read. I am in trouble, and I do not know what to do or how to handle it."

I started to read the letter, and I was shocked. It was from a woman telling him that she wanted to move to New York and live with him. He told me she was the one who had come to New York days before; this was the new shoe lady. She had a nine-year-old daughter, and she wanted to move here.

I asked, "Well, Bud, how do you feel about her?"

He said, "I have known her some time through Allied Van Lines. She is working for a company in Pennsylvania. No, you are the only one I care about."

Whew!

"If you do not want her here, you'd better tell her, because with the way she is operating, you are going to have an Allied van in front of your door in a few days."

Talk about naive. I was surprised, since he was so savvy about so much in life. He took care of it, but I saw her many times after at Allied conventions. I swear she must have had an uncanny way of knowing our schedule. Of course, I had found out who she was.

I was invited to North Haven on all weekends, and it was always fun doing things I had never done before. I grew up so far away from the ocean or even large bodies of water, but I learned fast and loved going out 4:00 or 5:00 a.m. It was not a very good boat, and we could not go far—just mostly around the bay—but that was all right, as I did not know about the ocean, anyway. Sometimes we caught a lot of fish, sometimes none, but I loved the water and the beauty of the shoreline. I mostly loved the excitement of doing what I had never experienced before. I guess I was like a child looking at a world I did not know existed. I should have been scared, as I am not a good swimmer, but Bud had grown up around the water and made me feel very secure.

Bud called me one day and asked if I knew anyone who could get us tickets to a Sinatra show. I said, "I will try, but he's not in New York; he is in Philly."

I called my friend Saul Richman—Mr. Broadway—and asked if he could help. He said, "Nadine, where is he appearing?"

I said, "In Philly tomorrow night."

He laughed and said, "Thanks for the big notice, Nadine. How many tickets do you want?"

"Six."

"*Six tickets?*"

"Yes." Well, I was naive—but it is why he spent time with me. Everyone else was so wise, and I was still wide eyed about everything that went on in New York. But I did not realize what I was asking for.

He called me back in ten minutes and said, "Okay, they are in your name."

I called Bud and told him we had six tickets. He said, "What? *Six* tickets?"

"Yes. How many people do you know who want to ride a train to Philly to see Sinatra?"

Well, he pulled that many, and we got on the train with a jug of mixed drinks, laughing and having the time of our lives. Bud had many friends, so it was easy for him to get a group. Now this was a group that could laugh and enjoy each other and never worry about anything else when we were playing. We all had plenty of issues, but all were smart enough not to lay much on each other.

We got off the train, and all were in rare form. We went to the great old well-known Bookbinder's restaurant and barely got to the theater in time for the show. We got our tickets and followed the attendant down, down, down to first row front. We were practically on the stage. Bud turned to me and said, "Who the hell is this Saul Richman?"

What a show! And at the end, Frank leaned over and gave me his handkerchief. I have no idea what I did with it. Would that not be neat to have now?

Life was full in so many ways. Bud made me know that I was a worthy human being. He never asked why I'd stayed with Tom so long.

I loved my life, although I was missing so much with my own daughter. Bud's daughters were the same age as Mary, so I could kind of imagine how tall she was and how big. I had a great relationship with them.

A funny thing happened with them early on. Bud had skied in his early years but had given it up after his children were born and after he had acquired lots of business-related responsibility after his father died. He looked for things to do with the girls and decided to take them to learn to ski, and they were very excited. He asked me to join them.

This was very foreign to me. Being from Arkansas, we rarely saw even snow flurries, much less tons of snow. But I am always game for anything, so I went along. The girls and I used rented gear. I am athletic, but it was not at all feeling like something I was going to love doing.

There were no instructors, and I was looking at this little hill. I knew I was in the wrong place, but I'm not a quitter, and Bud gave a few instructions to us. Then the girls went down the hill, and I followed, falling as much as being upright.

They went up and down about four times, and then they were ready to join their dad. I started down the fourth time and headed straight toward a tree. I did not hit the tree, but limbs were hanging down, and I needed to stop, so I reached up and grabbed tree limbs. I was left swinging in the air and afraid to let go and put my feet down. I turned my head, hoping no one was watching. Sure enough, the three of them were at the top, laughing.

Enough, I thought. I let go. I laugh now to think what a sight I must have been. I landed and took off the skis and walked up the hill. "See you inside; this is not for me."

Bud apologized. He said it was icy, but did not want disappoint the girls.

Shortly after, he took to me to Chanteclair, Quebec, in Canada, where the snow was just great. I spent the mornings in lessons and then practiced all afternoon. I would go back to the condo and a fire would be going and a glass of wine poured for me. I would be exhausted but happy that I was learning. By the end of the week, we had our little race down to get our certificate with our numbers on our chests. I went all the way down and did not fall.

I could now say I knew how to ski. I knew it was not going to be my sport. Bud knew it too. He very shortly said, "You know, my ankles hurt. I think I am going to give up trying to ski anymore." The gentleman as always. The girls kept it up.

Bud loved piano bars if there was great music. A favorite spot was Jilly's. Celebrities were always there—Sinatra, Judy Garland, Ray Charles, and many others—and therefore, each night was a surprise. We went there very often and had many memorable nights.

Bobby Cole, who played there nightly, was always great to listen to. Any time we went in, he played a song called "You Could Hear a Pin Drop" that was to us our song; it was if he had written for us.

Frank Sinatra, as all know, was a showman of all times. We went to Vegas to see him many times. The one that blew everyone away was at Forest Hills Stadium. He flew in by helicopter. He landed and swaggered across with his music under arm. The crowd went wild. What an evening.

Another funny story was when we were in Vegas and Sinatra was playing at the Sands, where he most often played. Bud knew Sam, the manager of the men's club, and he always let them in when Sinatra and all the others were there—Dean Martin, Sammy Davis, Nat King Cole, and others of the entertainment world—because they would never bother them and just be little flies on the wall. The club closed down for them.

Now these fellows evidently loved to play jokes on each other, and one evening, it was just before Sinatra was going on stage. He was having a steam bath. His handler was there, and they all decided to play a joke on Frank. There was just time for him to dress, and when his handler was giving him his clothes, he said, "Oh Lord, Frank, I forgot your shorts." There was no time to go to his room to get them. Frank sang that performance with no shorts on. They thought it was so funny.

There was a time when they heard Nat King Cole say before going on that he was so tired and he did not know why. He died within two months of cancer.

One evening in the late '60s, we had gone to a Broadway show, and afterward, we came upon a large circle of people who had gathered around something. Of course, we stopped to see what was going on. It was a man and a woman in the middle of the circle, and he was beating this woman up something terrible. Here were all these people watching and doing nothing to help her. This was in the days when women were carrying large purses much like today. This was too much for me to see. I ran into the middle and started hitting this man with all my might with my handbag. Every swing I made was for Tom, the ones I did not give to him. He ran like a thief. The crowd cheered and laughed. I looked around and saw men who had done nothing; they had just watched this woman being punched like in a boxing match.

Bud was shocked by what I did. He said, "I guess all of us men did not react the way we should have."

I said, "That is just the way it is, but not with me there. Never would I let that happen to anyone else."

He asked me if I had been afraid since the man could have had a knife or gun. I told him that I had no fear, as I had learned from my own experience, and that men like him are cowards who only pick on women—never another man. But even if he *had* had a weapon, as a human being and having been in that woman's situation, I had to react.

Bud asked me to meet him and Tom O'Donnell at Jack Dempsey's restaurant on Broadway and Fiftieth one afternoon. Of course, I went, as they were always up to something and usually fun. I went in, and the big surprise was that they were sitting with the great prizefighter Jack Dempsey. I of course remembered the days of his fighting, and he was the best. When I looked at his hands, I understood why. Any man could put his hands side by side and that was how big his hands were. He had a very soft voice, which was the opposite of his other persona. My daddy would have loved to have met him and could probably have told him of each of his fights, as he never missed listening to all of them on the radio.

I had not seen Mary in a number of years, having no idea where she was and having tried every way, with lawyers trying to track her and her father down without success. I then got a call from Tom. Mary was thirteen at the time.

It was the worst call of all calls. He told me that Mary was in the hospital and that she had taken an overdose of pills. She was in intensive care, and the doctors had to do a tracheotomy and did not think she was going to live. "You need to get here," he said.

I started to shake badly. "Where?"

He told me that Mary was in a Catholic hospital in Cleveland, Ohio. I hung up to call Inez but was shaking so much that I could not dial the number. I got the operator on the line, and she dialed it for me. I called Henry Clay because he was always so helpful. He told me to take all pertinent information. Thank God I had her birth certificate and my marriage and divorce papers showing that I had custody.

I should have questioned whether Tom was trying to upset me with another one of his big, cruel lies, but I did not.

How I got there I do not know; everything is blocked in my mind. This horror was too much to even consider. I arrived and went to the hospital desk and asked for Mary. A man looked up from the desk and asked, "Who are you?"

"Her mother."

He said, "It says here the mother is deceased."

I said, "Who is in charge of the hospital? Get her to come down here."

In came the nun in the uniform of the day. She talked to me, and I explained to her what she was dealing with. I opened my suitcase that was sitting on the floor and pulled out all the papers. She read the papers and looked at me and said, "Your daughter is in bad shape."

I said, "He told me she has had a tracheotomy."

She said, "She has not had one."

I looked at her in disbelief, but why should have I been surprised?

She said, "I will take you up, but you can only stay a few minutes. She is in critical condition, but she will wake up. I do not know how she will react."

I told them of Mary being abducted from me against my wishes for a few long years. I was, of course, now crying, and I tried to pull myself together. We went up, and they woke her. She had tubes all over.

She would not talk to me, and I understood why. How could she know the pain I had and how much I loved her, especially feeling how badly I had failed her?

I called my brother Ralph in Little Rock and asked him to come to Cleveland, and he did. I got a room in a hotel close by and stayed away until my brother got there. I could not deal with Tom at that point, and I knew he would be looking for me. I did not need to hear any of his stories.

When Ralph arrived, I told him all about the call from Tom and then my experience with the hospital. Ralph, poor innocent one. He said, "You must have misunderstood him; that would be so mean."

I said, "That is what I have dealt with all these years. He *is* that mean."

Tom walked into the hospital waiting room where Ralph and I were as if everything was okay between us and asked us to go the chapel to pray. I said, "No. I pray wherever I am."

My brother is very involved in his church, so it is natural for him to go to the chapel. I did not want to try to explain to Ralph at that point all that was going on.

Tom probably never said a prayer in his life. I prayed, but it was for Tom to drop dead so I could take my daughter and get help.

They did a test on her and said there had been sexual activity.

I ask to see the sister in charge, and I told her, "Listen to me: he is a very mentally disturbed man. I have no proof, but who but him? You must listen to me. Tom is a very difficult person. You have seen enough of him with what has happened in the last few days that you need to be very concerned. I am sure he has lied about several things as he always does."

She said, "Yes, we have many concerns." They had tried to talk to Mary, but she would not say, and they had no solid proof. Why would she? She had to be very scared of him if I was as an adult.

They told me I had one choice since I had custody. I would have to file papers in the courts, and since she did not want to go with me, the courts would put her in a children's home.

I could not fathom a father being responsible for sexual abuse. However, all signs pointed to him.

It was a very difficult decision, as it meant her being taken into custody, but I knew it would be better in the long run. No one should have to make such a choice. When would the madness ever end for her and me? I was an adult, and I could not protect her.

Never did I blame her for refusing to talk. As an adult, I had been fearful of him, so she had to be so scared of him too. Many years later, she confirmed his abuse. I would like to think there are no longer such things happening, but I know they do.

It was reported to child services. They did not let her go home with him, and she refused me. She was put in a children's home. Now my real fights began.

I hired a lawyer and made many trips to Ohio. I talked to the director of the home and on a daily basis to her social workers. I had gone to court, and the judge said, "She does not belong with her father, but she does not want to go with you." I still have a letter from the judge explaining to me that someday she would grow up and be able to make better decisions and come to me. I made many trips to see her, and they would make her come in along with her counsel, but it always the same; she would not talk.

I sent gifts, but she acknowledged none of them. I even sent gifts at Christmas for all the other kids, thinking they might not have anything.

I could not believe he had visitations. Then they let her go to his apartment for visits. Of course, I am sure he had put the pressure on her to request it. He did not give up, but I understand why. He needed to keep control, as she might have finally admitted his behavior in therapy.

I spent lots of money and time on trips and felt I got nowhere. I always came back so disheartened. Sometimes my mind was so far away, but Bud was always willing to listen, though he felt very helpless to change things. He was the most caring husband, but of course, this was an impossible situation that no one could change, it seemed.

I was now supporting Bud with his issues with Vicki when she came to live with us, although her situation was dramatically improving.

Time passed with no improvement in my relationship with Mary.

Mary remained in the children's home until she was eighteen when she had to be released. She still would not come with me, and the courts would not let her go with her father.

For all those years, I made trips to see her, but she would never talk to me. There is no doubt he was telling her lies about me when he visited her. They had to let her see him if she said she wanted to.

Those were very trying years for me. While all this was happening, I was married and living with Bud, Vicki, and Valerie in New York. I was so happy with Bud, but my mind was constantly on Mary. I felt there had to be some way to break this cycle of Tom's control.

I long ago started doing my own investments and made money in the markets with the help of Hugh Cassel, the stockbroker. I was very fortunate in meeting Mr. Cassel; he owned a brokerage firm. I had dinner with his family every Wednesday night for several years. His daughter, Lenore, his ex-wife, Lady Tucker, and her husband, Sir Tucker, were there many times, and it made for very interesting conversations.

Lenore was my age had lived a totally different life from mine. I actually felt lucky when I sat at dinner with them. They had money, but I had so much more of the real important things. She had three children and never needed to work outside the home. She was so lovely, but her life was not a happy one.

Mr. Cassel was now in his eighties and had no one to take over the brokerage firm. He started to put pressure on her to start working with him. She had just inherited from two aunts in Mexico. I was told they were leaving her $20 million. She also stood to receive not only his money but, as an only child, her mother's. Of course, she had no desire to work with him and had her children to raise. She had a husband I never met, whom she later divorced.

We had many dinners together, and he began to compare her to me—specifically that I was eager to learn, and she did not want to. He spoke of how I did want to learn about finance, and I did learn from him. I started to put money into the market instead of savings accounts. I asked many questions. I went to his office to watch the old ticker tapes. This comparison was very embarrassing to me, and one evening, she got up from the table and ran out of the room crying.

I stood up and said, "Do not ever compare Lenore to me. You have placed her where she is today. If you ever compare us again, I will never sit at your table again. Go apologize to your daughter." He did.

When she divorced her husband, I introduced her to my friend Henry Clay. He was so much fun, and I thought he would at least make her a nice escort, and he loved life. I thought it would lighten up her life.

Well, that did not work. She and I were having lunch, and she told me she would never marry another who did not have as much as she did. I laughed and said, "Lenore, you just ruled out with those odds of ever being married again."

I was dating Bud at the time. Mr. Cassel now started asking me to come into his office. He wanted to teach me the market so that I could take over his business. I said no. He was smart, but he would dominate my life, and I did not want that. It was a great opportunity for me, but I knew it had many pitfalls. So instead, I learned from him.

I saved his life one night when I was having dinner with him alone and his cook, Ida, had made chicken. We were eating, and all of a sudden, he was choking. He was a very short man and did not weigh much. I jumped up and began beating on his back. Nothing happened, so I put my arms under his ribs and lifted. Up came a chunk of chicken.

Ida never heard a thing from the kitchen. If I had not been there, he would have choked to death.

He taught me so much during those years of friendship. He was also very generous at Christmas—he gave me shares in companies. He affected my life by giving me the opportunity to have money to continue my business at a much faster pace.

To my amazement, when he died, I got a letter from his attorney to come and sign off on papers. He had left me $25,000. That was a lot of money to me. I put it in the stock market. It was my way of making the most of his generosity.

He would have approved.

CHAPTER 7

To the Good Times

The night Bud asked me to marry him was crazy. In three years, we had never talked about marriage—and remember I had told him that I would never marry again that first month we met.

It was 1967, and we went to a friend's yacht in Pelham and had a really good time. Driving back down the FDR to Manhattan, he said, "I have something very important I want to talk to you about tonight."

I said, "So what is it?"

He said, "Let's stop at Johnny's Bar." It was just down from his apartment and was a neighborhood hangout. We parked the car and went in and ordered drinks.

Bud downed one drink very quickly, and I said, "What is it?" He ordered another Dewar's and water.

After he had two, I said, "Okay, let's hear what is so hard for you to say." I was a little concerned because we had always been able to communicate without holding back.

I could not believe it when he said, "Let's talk about it tomorrow."

I said, "It's that bad you cannot say it now? And you expect me to go home to my apartment wondering why you are so nervous? This was in the days when it was uncommon, and even frowned upon, to live with someone before you were married.

I assumed it must have been bad, and I was wondering, *What gives?*

He asked me to go up to his apartment. It was now almost 2:00 a.m. *Let's get it over with*, I thought. *He must have met someone else. What else could it be?*

We went, and he turned on Sinatra and poured us drinks. He came around the bar and said, "Let's dance." At that point, I thought, *This is getting crazy.*

I was ready to say, "Forget about the drama; I am going home."

He took a few steps, pushed me back, and said, "How would you like to spend the rest of your life with me?"

"Are you asking me to marry you?"

"Yes."

I said, "I'll have to think about it."

It sure did not take me long—about five seconds. *Are you out of your mind, Nadine?* I thought. *You are so in love but have refused to believe anyone would love you and treat you with so much love and respect.* So I immediately said yes.

I never regretted a moment.

I wish everyone could have that kind of marriage, as it never wavered. So many people stay together who are unhappy. They do not realize they would be doing a favor to the other person to be honest. You should always know the second time what you really want and expect of a relationship. There's no rush if it's love; it will last through a couple of years getting to know each other. Hopefully, most know the first time. If the relationship does not last—and many do not—then it certainly would have been a bad marriage. There's a huge difference between lust and love; in fact, the only ways they are alike is that both are four-letter words starting with an *L*. If you can have both together, that is the ultimate marriage. Otherwise, save a lawyers' fee and a lot of hurt feelings.

That was such a happy time for us. We had both gotten over any concerns we might have had over marriage, me especially. I now found myself not afraid to admit I truly loved him and trusted him and that I wanted to be with him for the rest of my life.

Bud and I decided we were going to keep it secret.

I gave Bud a surprise birthday party on December

12—the same as Sinatra's birthday—and it was a blast. I invited his mother and other relatives and many friends. When the crowd thinned out, we went to Danny's Hideaway for a dinner even though I had served lots of food.

We all partied hard in those days. We called ourselves long-ball hitters. We had plenty to drink.

At the restaurant, Bud leaned over and said to me, "I have to tell my friends. I am so happy."

I said, "No, it's to be a surprise." I pulled on his pants leg, but up he went. There were about ten people, and not only did he tell them but he also said, "If you want to come to Vegas for the wedding, you are all invited."

The calls came in. They were all coming along. Bud was in a dither. February 2, 1968, was the date. It was mid-December, and we had all the plans already made—the airline tickets, chapel, hotel, and wedding dinner were all planned. We did all this without telling many other people, but we planned to have a party when we got back to tell all.

For the trip to Vegas, we arrived at LaGuardia, and there were ten of us for the United Flight 711. It was a late-night flight, and there were maybe four other people on the plane with us.

In the bar at the airport, we had a ball, and Inez and

her girlfriend Bobbie Rudolph were laughing so hard about how they were both going to meet rich Texans and get married too.

Well, while we were laughing, a big six-foot-five guy passed the bar going to a gate. He had a big cowboy hat, boots, and a white beard, and we kidded them about which one was going to run after Tex.

We got on the plane, and forty-five minutes out, the flight attendants brought folded newspapers and handed them out to each of us. I opened it, and it was a fake paper with headlines that read SCHRAMM DOES IT AGAIN AND SALB THINKS HE'S NUTS.

Tom Salb was a neighbor in North Haven who said they could not make the flight. So we figured he just pulled a joke on us.

At about that time, the tall man in the airport, whom we had assumed was a Texan, came up to us. It was actually Tom Salb. No one had recognized him earlier. He hid on the plane out of view until that very moment. I immediately realized who it was. Then the party went crazy. The flight attendants were in on it too.

By the time we got to Vegas, we had consumed all the booze for a full planeload. The pilot came back, and though he did not drink, he became part of the party.

Getting off the plane, I was carrying my gown, and

Tom Powers took it. At that time, to go to the terminal in Vegas, there was an escalator. Tom got on, and the next thing I knew, he was sliding down the escalator handrail with my dress bag under him. I was mortified, thinking that my dress was ruined. I checked it, and nothing had happened to it. Amazing.

We invited the crew to come to the pool at our hotel the next day, which was Caesars Palace. Oh, was it grand back then. It had just opened. They came. They all said it was the most memorable flight they had ever had. They recognized us as well as our guests for several years.

The trip and plans for the wedding in Vegas were something else. Bud had to get limos and flowers and up the party to thirteen. Three came from California to meet us. We had to meet the minister of Chapel of the Bells, who kept us for two hours just talking to us. He said, "I have married many people before you. I have never felt quiet as strong as I do about the two of you. I am so sure you are going to be forever the happiest of the ones I will ever marry."

The wedding was so beautiful. Not a dry eye. They all knew how much we loved each other and had watched the love grow. Anyone who knew us knows the minister's prediction came totally to pass.

Well, the dinner was fabulous with a waiter wearing

white gloves behind each person. Nubian girls held on their shoulders wine in gallon jugs and fed grapes soaked in wine one at a time to the men. They loved it, and it was a sight. What a time we had there.

We went on to San Francisco and Carmel by the seventeen-mile coastline drive. Our good friends Jack and Hilda went with us. They are like family, so we knew it would just add to the fun having them with us, and it did.

Carmel is a beautiful small town, and we so enjoyed the seventeen-mile ride up with the views that are just unbelievable.

We came back through Arkansas for Bud to meet the Shelby family and celebrate our marriage. When my father answered the door, he greeted Bud with "I am the chief. Welcome." I think he was taking no chance of Bud not knowing that he was someone still looking over my choice. I had never heard him use that statement before, and I laughed, as did Bud.

They had a party for us, and Bud came home to New York, making me repeat all the names, and he tried to remember them all, which is impossible with my big family; sometimes I have to struggle to remember the younger ones. He was from a very small family.

My father had started teaching Sunday school lessons at the Methodist church to the young men when they moved in to town. My mother read him the Bible, and he would then in his mind plan for the Sunday church lessons. There always seemed to be someone coming to talk to my dad. Later, they talked about how he had affected their lives. They could come and talk to him so openly when they could not with their parents. Six of these men were pallbearers at his funeral. Several told of his ability to make them understand the important things in life. He was never judgmental of anyone.

Bud and I were at Jilly's many nights, but one night stands out as one of the most memorable. I sat on a bar stool next to Judy Garland the night before she did her last show at the Palace Theatre, that grand old theater on Broadway. Bobby Cole, who played piano at Jilly's, was her producer and pianist for that show. She was so tiny that all I could think of was a sparrow. She was very friendly, and we talked a bit. I told her how much we had enjoyed her for so many years and that we would be there the next night cheering her on. She sang so beautifully at that last show. Then she went to Europe, where she died such a short time later.

Bud and I made a trip to Florida. Bud had heard about a new kind of boat that was unsinkable, called a MAKO, and it sounded good to me. We went to the factory to see how they were made. They were new, and Bud fell in love with them; they were fiberglass and filled with a foam that was sprayed into the hull. That little boat of his was getting to me, so I told him, "Let's buy it."

This one was twenty-two feet, and it could go into the ocean and way out if we had twin engines. No problem. Bud had a friend with Evinrude Motors who could get twin 85s shipped to us in New Jersey, where the MAKO dealership was.

Now Bud, Jack Kirkeby, and I were going to take that boat out to Sag Harbor. It happened to be during the big gas crisis. The dealer had promised Bud he would give us enough to get to Sag.

He had given us just enough to get us up the river where he told us we would be able to get some more. Well, we had to beg, but finally the man filled us up.

It was a beautiful day with great sunshine. We got into New York Harbor in the shipping lanes where all cruise ships and tankers go through. There was fog, and we could not see five feet in front of us. We could hear the foghorns from the buoys and the huge boats. It had been so nice. Bud, who was usually prepared, had just brought along a small compass.

Bud got us to the buoy and said that we were just going to circle until the fog lifted. I was to lie on the bow and tell him if he made a move away. I was scared and hollered out. Who the hell needs to buy this kind of problem?

Jack wore glasses, and they were fogging up. The fog lifted a little, and Bud said, "I am making a run for Rockaway Inlet." He had flown small airplanes, so he knew the patterns for the planes going to John F. Kennedy International Airport, which was the direction we needed to go.

Well, the fog was getting heavy again, so he had trouble finding the inlet. Suddenly, we came upon a man fishing. We pulled to his side, and Bud asked, "Do you know where the inlet is?"

The fisherman said, "You are in it."

We went on and came to a motel and boat dock. It was getting late and foggier, and we knew there was probably no way for us to reach Sag before night. We decide to stay at the motel for the night.

It was a great idea, but when we tied up and went in to ask for rooms, they were sold out because of a big wedding party, and the restaurant was also booked.

We told him our problems, and the clerk said, "Look, I have two rooms that I was holding for overflow from the wedding, but I will give them to you. You do not have transportation to go eat, and it is too far to walk; let me see what I can do. The wedding has the dining room for the night."

He left for a moment and then returned, saying, "I

just talked to the bride and groom, and they said you will join their party."

"We have only the clothes on our backs," I said.

"I told them that is probably the case. They said it would add flavor to their party."

We showered and put on smiles and our messed-up clothes. The day had gotten much better!

The next thing we knew, we were drinking champagne, and we had a beautiful dinner. Some people are very generous to people in distress.

One time, Bud, Tom, and I were fishing on the point off Shelter Island. It was a feeding frenzy with fish. We were all doing great, standing knee deep. They Bud and Tom moved to shore to remove their catch. I was still standing knee deep in the water, casting. Three feet in front of me went two fins about four feet apart. Though I have none of those special skills, I nevertheless either walked or ran on water. If that shark did not think the fish looked better than my legs, I would not be walking around in high heels every day.

A few days later, Chris Salb and some of the young boys went shark hunting where we had been fishing. A couple of days later, they got the shark. Boy, it was one big sucker.

Bud and I decided to have a party in our beach house

on North Haven, Long Island. This one was going to be different. We had lots of parties there, because it was so easy and on the water, which we all loved. It was also away from anyone who might complain of noise.

Everyone was to dress in costumes. Well, it was a sight to behold. Bud dressed as Fidel Castro, complete with beard and rubber chicken and a military service uniform. This was several years after Fidel had been in New York in 1959, and he had kept live chickens in his hotel room up in Harlem. Fidel was at the United Nations for meetings in 1959. It was his first, and I know it was his last. It was in the news every day.

I am not sure how I got this idea go to Kraft Foods, but I have a tendency to think out of the box, and I sure did on this one. I went to their office on Lexington Avenue and asked if I could borrow their Mr. Peanut costume for the weekend. They wanted to know if it would be used in any way with advertising or in public, and I assured them that it was just for a private party. Much to my surprise, they let me have it.

Well, it was one of the most fun-filled parties ever. All our friends were very creative. The group was all our friends from North Haven. Bud and I won the prize for being most creative. Our group played hard, but we also worked at a fast pace all week, so we needed to have fun-filled weekends.

Inez retired some months later and moved back to Arkansas. She had longtime friends Bill McMinn and his wife, Mary Ann, who visited her in Fort Smith and fell in love with Arkansas. Bill was a retired pilot from TWA. He had learned to fly as a kid in the fields in Michigan. He flew the first double-deck TWA plane before he retired. Bud flew with him to Vegas on it. Bud was thrilled to be able to see that cockpit, which was a lot different from the little plane he flew.

Bill and Mary Anne ended up buying a home in Fort Smith, and Inez went to their house for dinner. Another couple was there whom she did not know. They were introduced, and it came out in conversation that I was Inez's sister.

Don't you know, it was the SOB who had fired me from Arkansas Medical Society, and he was with his wife. She was in a wheelchair. I told my sister, "I hope he has to push her around a long time." It is strange for me to say something like that, as I am not a person who holds grudges, but he had been over the top with my firing. She died a few months later, I was sorry to hear.

Now Inez saw him, and he was with another woman. This woman said she worked with me. I had told Inez the story about him firing me, and I made a remark that was very unusual for me—"Did he ever grow balls?" Who was his companion? It was the woman who was previously referred to as Mousy.

Now it all came together for me. He must have been having an affair with her, and the wife knew he was cheating and just assumed it would be the divorcée. I laughed. I had seen his wife a couple of times when she came to the office, and she was a very pretty woman. He had to cover, and I guess the wife thought the problem had been taken care of. I was the fall person.

I have been able to laugh at this, and at the time, I told my sister to make sure she let him know I could buy everything he had and have some left over. Also I had someone who would never cheat on me as he did his wife.

Well, of course I am sure she did not elaborate, but she did let him know I had moved on.

Bud's ex-wife had sold the house in New Jersey after their divorce and moved in with his daughters, Valerie and Vicki, to her mother's in Southampton. Valerie had adapted well and made good grades, but Vicki was not happy. She was younger, and the divorce had affected her probably more, as she was Daddy's little girl.

Vivian, the ex-wife, had bought a restaurant in Southampton, Long Island, with a fellow, and she was out early in the morning and then did not get home until after midnight. The grandmother had the responsibility of seeing that they got to school and did homework. Budd and I did not feel the grandmother should be taking care of them; she did not want that much time with them. For many years, she had lived alone. To have two depend on her for all was not feasible.

Vivian called Bud and said she could not handle Vicki and asked if she could send Vicki to live with us.

Bud said, "I will have to ask Nadine; she will be the one who will have the larger share of daily care." Of course I said yes.

These were in the times of drugs running rampant. Of course, Southampton, with all the money, was a good place to sell. Vicki had been trying a little marijuana, and that was a real no-no. She would go in to her mother and say she did not feel well when it was time to go to school. It was easy to just let her stay home.

Now I had the job of finding a school, and the first thing I found was the City of New York had started the program of switching kids of out their neighborhoods. If she went to a public school, Vicki would have ended up in Harlem or the Lower East Side, and these were not good options for a child already having problems.

I went to Saint Vincent Ferrer High School and asked to see the sister in charge. I told her the story of Vicki's problem and that her father trusted me to find the school, and I felt very comfortable doing it. The big question from the sister was "Are you Catholic?"

I said, "She is; I am not. Sister, she is one of yours. She needs help badly. She is not a bad child; she is just lost in her environment. Her father, of course, was divorced, so you know the story there."

She said, "You are unusual that you, a stepmother, seem to be taking this major project on, and it will not be easy. I cannot believe you came to me as a non-Catholic."

I said, "It is the place she needs to be." I told her I had handled harder things.

She said, "Get me all her school records, report cards, and attendance records."

I told Bud to call the ex and have the records overnighted to me. She was very happy to do so.

I saw the records and wondered how I would pull it off. Vicki had failing grades and a 50 percent attendance rate. I went up for my appointment with the sister, and she looked at the records, looked up at me, and said, "This is a mess." I agreed.

She said, "This attendance record really worries me."

I said, "Sister, she will be here every day. I guarantee you she will be here on time every day. She will not miss one day of school unless she is ill—and I do mean *ill*."

Sister said, "Bring her in; I want to meet her."

I told Vicki where we are going, and she had a fit. "I am not going to a Catholic school and wear those plaid uniforms!" she said.

I said, "You are going. Now I will take you and show you the places you would be assigned to if you go to public school. This is not Southampton. You have already blown that. You think you would survive one semester in Harlem? You are a spoiled brat. Get over it. Do you know how hard I have had to work to give you the opportunity to get in this school?"

Vicki went for the interview. First, both of us were invited in, and then I was asked to leave. I was not sure if Vicki was going to blow it. Later, the sister invited me back in alone. She said, "This is one big gamble on her. But I admire what you are doing, and I am counting on you."

I said, "I will not let you down. She will be here on time. She will do her homework, and I will work with her."

Then we had to get the required uniforms, and she was not happy. I said, "You will learn to like it—no worrying about what to wear every day. One thing at a time, of course, but I am thinking you might as well throw out those torn blue jeans."

She tried me a couple of times with pretending to be sick. I said, "You go, and if you still do not feel well at noontime, have Sister call me, and I will come and pick you up." I never had the call.

I think it might have had something to do with embarrassment of her stepmother picking her up at her age. She graduated and never missed a day.

In 1972, Mary was eighteen and out of the court system, so they asked me if I would agree for her to go to Texas to live with her aunt Jayne, Tom's sister. It was not what I wanted, but since she would not come with me, it was the best that could be done. Mary was finally not with her father or me but with Aunt Jayne and Uncle Jay, who had been so good to me in Irving, Texas. I trusted them, as they were very upstanding people, and it was very generous of them to take the responsibility of her.

She was now old enough to get a job. She did and seemed to be doing well, and I was thankful she was in a stable home.

Tom, the bad nickel, went back to Texas. As always, he again took control. His sister did not resist, and Mary was out of the Ohio court system. Tom took her to Cleveland again. I could not believe it. She got a job in Cleveland, but luck never seemed to be on her side.

She got in an automobile accident. She had gotten in a car to get home with a girl she was working with who wanted to stop by a bar on their way home. Mary did not drink and shortly wanted to go home, but her friend wanted to stay. So the friend introduced her to a young man who was going to leave, and he said that he would drop her off, so she went with him. He was from a well-known family, and I tried to get them to be responsible for the medical bills later, but of course, their connections worked against any help.

She knew she had to be home, as her father would be mad. She got in the car, and after one block at a stoplight, she realized he'd had too much to drink, and she asked to get out. He took off to the ramp for the expressway and ran off the ramp into a light pole. She was taken to the hospital with lots of damage to her hip. She was there for quite some time before I knew. When I found out, I went to the Cleveland hospital to see her.

She didn't talk much, but at least she knew I cared enough to go there. Some months later, there was a lawsuit. I hired an attorney for her and made trips out to Cleveland. I was a mother seeking to get justice, but there would be none. My money was taken by the lawyer, and she got almost nothing. And the medical bills were substantial. She was on crutches for many months, and I felt so helpless, knowing things had to be so hard for her. It was so hard to work on it from such a distance. Then I got the call I had waited for.

CHAPTER 8
My Prayers Answered

On a Friday, Bud and I arrived in North Haven, and Denise was very upset. She had gotten a call from Mary asking for me. She was at the airport in Cleveland. They would not take her check for a plane ticket to New York. She had asked for me to call her and left the number of the airport manager. As it turned out, she had gone to the airport manager and told him that she was running from her father and needed to get to New York. I talked to him, and since it was before the days of credit cards, I said to him, "If you are an airport manager, you must be old enough to have children, so you can imagine how I feel. I need to get her to New York."

He says, "Well, we do not have another plane till morning."

I said, "She is only eighteen years old. Please put her in a hotel room by the airport and get her a ticket. You will get a check or money order from me right away. Please trust me. She is in danger."

He said, "Do not worry; I will take care of it." He did, and I sent him the money with a big thank-you. Bud and I went back to the city to be there when she arrived.

She came, and I was so happy. She told me later that she was so nervous not knowing what Bud would be like. She said the minute she saw the smile on his face, she knew she would be fine.

Mary shared the twin bedroom with Vicki. The first night, I knew all would be well when I heard them giggling at one in the morning. I was so happy. Finally, she was with us, and she had accepted my family. Vicki was seventeen, and Mary was eighteen.

Mary went to work in Bud's office on crutches and worked there for some time. She got a job elsewhere, as Bob Schramm was not happy that she was there, and he made it difficult for her. Bob had three daughters, and they lived way out on Long Island. One had worked two days and quit. He just did not want my daughter there.

Mary is very smart and fit right in. Another reason was Denise, Bud and Bob's mother, spent a great deal of time with Mary playing Scrabble, and she really enjoyed spending time with her. None of her other granddaughters spent any time with her doing things as Mary did.

A new job was a good move for her. She met new people. She lived with us, and all was well. She and Bud got along great, and she and I were close for the first time in all those years. She went to the country with us every weekend, and she and Denise had a wonderful relationship. Denise treated her as her own granddaughter, and Mary thrived. They also played backgammon together and were always laughing.

I had stock in her name that I had bought for her over the years. She cashed it and bought her car; it was her first major purchase. She loved driving out to the country and the freedom it gave her.

Things were going well with no problems. She confirmed that her father had abused her and that it was the reason she had tried to take her life. She thrived in her new life, and all was well.

At about that time, Bud told me of a sailboat he had seen, and I listened and knew this was something he had always dreamed of. When he was very young, he had taken sailing lessons. He came home and said he had seen the most beautiful sailboat down at South Street Seaport. It had been crushed by a barge, and several ribs were badly damaged. Now I could tell there was more to this story. I asked him what the owner was going to do. Would he repair it?

Bud said, "No, he wants to sell it."

I said, "So that must be the reason you were there. So what is the deal?"

Tom Salb had called him and asked him if he would go down with him to see this old schooner.

The *Eskasoni* was an exact replica of the *Bluenose*, one of the best racing schooners ever built. Both were built in Nova Scotia in the early 1900s, and both were wooden.

I asked how much it cost, and he said it was too much and that it would be expensive to rebuild the ribs. I said, "Well, this is something you have dreamed of, so what is the big deal?"

Tom wanted us to be partners. I told him he would always regret not doing it. I said I would put up the money. It would be his Christmas gift or whatever. He was like a kid, so we bought it.

We had her taken to a boatyard, and the ribs were repaired in Westchester. Then it was out to Sag Harbor to a boatyard. We had her hauled, and then our hard work began. What fun it was. Every weekend, we worked—and I mean a hard labor of love. Finally, it was time for the first outing, and she was a beauty. Everyone was excited about the addition to the harbor.

The Salbs had a sailboat before, but it was much

smaller, so we decided to motor over to Dering Harbor on Shelter Island. We spent the night aboard, and the next morning, we got up to go back to Sag.

She was a fifty-seven-foot vessel, and that was one big boat for that harbor. Tom announced he was sailing out of the harbor.

Bud said no way. Tom Salb's wife, Audrey, also said no. I did not know anything at that point about sailing, so I was quiet, but I knew I trusted Bud's judgment, and he was not happy.

Tom was insistent that he knew how to sail her out, and he started pulling up sails. Tom was a tall and very macho man who did what he wanted. Bud knew he had to do something, and Tom went back to the wheel.

One sail was now up, but the wind filled it up fast. We were moving toward a small moored motorboat. There was no room to jibe or do anything. We were going to ram the smaller boat. Bud and I ran forward to try to stave off. Tom had now run from the wheel and was absolutely screaming, "Oh my God! I am going to kill all those people!" He had totally lost it.

In the meantime, one of the metal stays had wrapped around the wheel and had it locked in position. Bud and I ran back to the wheel to try to release it. Nothing happened. As we hit, the impact caused the sail to release some of the wind, which in turn gave some give on the stay, and we were able to release it.

Bud turned the engine on and backed off. Now the man, as you can imagine, was in a total panic. His wife and two children were down below. Thank God they were all right. We gave the man all our information and told him we would take care of damages. We paid the bill when it was repaired, and it was small.

We did not sail out of that harbor. Tom tried to make us promise that we would not tell that story to anyone. Bud laughed and told him, "How many schooners do you think are named the *Eskasoni*, and how many boats that big try to sail out of a small harbor? Before we get back to Sag Harbor, it will be the talk of the town."

Bud was very unhappy. If this was any indication of the way she was to be sailed, he knew disaster would strike again.

I do not think Tom tried to sail out of any other harbor. We had so much fun on her, and we did not have any disasters. However, we did have another big scene. Salb had sailed up to Newport, and we were going to sail her back. Now there was a hurricane warning, but we went on up, thinking the storm might pass. Our friends Paul and Irene Kenwood flew down from Montreal to New York, and we were joined by Jack and Hilda Kirkeby. We drove to Newport and realized that the storm was going to hit.

Instead of staying on the boat, we rented motel rooms on the water so we could do watch. Jack and Bud were real boatmen, so they started tying up for the storm. They started crisscrossing lines from pilings on either side. Lots of line was put out.

By then, all the other boatmen were watching. They had not been watching the weather and thought we were just tying in for the night. They started laughing and telling the boys, "This is a safe harbor—why so many lines?"

Bud told them the hurricane would hit within so many hours and that they should tie before it hit. Needless to say, they did not. You should have seen them trying once it hit. They were jumping into the water in very heavy winds trying to pull lines across as we had in good weather. Bud and Jack stood on the sidelines thinking, *I told you so.*

That night, it was blowing a gale. Jack, Bud, and I decided to go up to town. As usual, I was not going to miss seeing what was happening.

I knew there would be no sleep. We did not walk—we were *blown* up there. We stopped in a local bar where there was a pool table. The local shark asked the guys if they would like to play. They pretended they did not want to . . .

well, just a little friendly game. Within five minutes, the locals wanted a bet.

The boys got serious, and they started winning. I was not so sure I liked this scene. The Newport guys were pretty rugged looking. Was I going to be backup for Jack and Bud? Well, we left with us laughing all the way back to the motel. It must have been the weather that kept those yokels from following us out to get their money back. I do not remember the amount they won, but it lightened up our evening.

Now we had to figure how we were going to get the *Eskasoni* back to Sag. We knew the seas would be rough, but she was big, and we decided to give it a try, so the next day, we led the way out.

Newport Harbor has a small inlet, and all the little boats were following us out. We just got out, and it was really rough. I saw Bud tense up, and I edged my way up to the wheel. He asked me, "What do you think? Should we go forward, as it will get better when we get to open seas, or should we go back?"

I said, "Well, we are close enough to shore to be picked up if the worst happens. Let's go back." I was already waving to small boats not to come out the inlet. I said, "I am afraid if we try, we will broach."

He said, "We may be better trying to make a large swing." That is what he did. That was the only time in all my sailing I thought I was going to get seasick, but I think it was fear. It was also the only time Bud showed any question of his ability.

We got back in safely. We knew we should leave the ship in Newport and go back the following weekend, as the seas would have calmed. We rented a car to go back to the city. Paul and Irene had left their suitcases in Sag, but they decided to go back to Montreal. They put their clothes in big black garbage bags, and we took them to the airport. What a sight, but we laughed about it many times. We went back the next weekend and sailed the *Eskasoni* back.

We went to Montreal, Canada, to see Paul and Irene Kenwood often, and they came to New York too. One of the trips was to a Grey Cup game—that is their big football game. We arrived at our hotel, and all the stores inside the hotel were boarded up. We asked why, but they were saving the story for us. It was because the fans from Calgary brought their horses with them on the train, and they rode them into the lobby of the hotel. We thought they were kidding, but they weren't. What a sight to see.

Those horses came right up the steps with cowboys, who had ridden the train all the way down. Yes, it was good reason for the store owners to cover their windows. It was a wild scene. They could have easily have backed into the glass on the store windows.

We were guests of Schenley Brewery and were taken to the games by limousine.

Trudeau was prime minister, and his wife had left him at the time. He sat just in front of us at the game. Women of Canada were crazy for him. He was like a rock star. His name was chanted all during the game. When the game was over, we went back to our limousine. Trudeau's car followed our caravan out of the stadium. The crowd went crazy, and they were rocking his car and all of ours. I was scared, but they were just having fun after too much of that beer.

Another one of those fun trips to Canada was when we went up for a big ball with Paul and Irene. We arrived after five o'clock, and the party was to be at seven o'clock that evening. That was a major problem for me, as my luggage did not arrive; I'd worn a suit with dress boots on the flight up. The stores were all closed, so there was no way to buy another gown. I was not going to cry over it or miss any party—especially that one.

I showered and put that suit right back on with the boots. It was one big party—cocktail hour, dinner, and then dancing. They had told everybody we were coming, and they introduced us around to the ones we did not know. Word traveled fast about my bags not arriving.

I had a ball that night, and I forever was remembered

when we went there as the one who had the best time of anyone in my suit and boots among all their gorgeous gowns. I danced all night. Some women, I am sure, would have stayed in their room, but not me.

I introduced Bud and Saul Richman. We spent a lot of time together and were invited to Saint Croix by Saul and Scarlet. They had a condo there in Estate Carlton Condos. We loved the island so much that we then rented a unit for a week from one of the owners. On the plane coming home, Bud said, "I love that island. It is so peaceful, and the local people are so pleasant." We loved their lilting voices.

One week later, I was on the phone with Scarlet asking if any of the units were for sale. She said yes. I said, "Tell me which ones." She told me of one owned by a young doctor and his wife. They had just adopted a newborn baby, and the condo did not fit in with their new lifestyle.

I got the telephone number and called the doctor. I asked the price, and he told me how much. I said, "Okay, I will send you $1,000 as a deposit, but I want to come down and see it. It is just a matter of the location of the unit. I do not care what or how it is decorated, as I will take care of that." Good thing I felt that way; it had dark carpet in an island condo. That was quick to go.

I walked into Bud's office and said, "I just bought a condo in the Estate Carlton Condos.

He said, "Are you kidding me?"

I told him I did, and he was thrilled. I told him, "I have to go back down to see it before paying for it."

He said, "I'm going too." We loved that place. We decorated it and went every time we could get away. We took Denise with us several times, and we invited Jack and Hilda. We also had the Kenwoods from Canada and Dottie and Bill Benisch from Newport, Rhode Island. What a crew. Again, we were long-ball hitters.

We were always doing crazy things to have a laugh. On one trip, Bill, being a big joker, was in the condo above ours, and from that patio, he got a rope and basket and lowered it to our patio with two glasses and a note that read "Please fill with scotch." Not a word said, scotch went in the glasses, and he pulled them up. What are good friends for?

Now I had a new interest that I was watching closely. Atlantic City had voted to get gambling, but it was turned down. I had strong feelings that the boys from Philadelphia would figure a way to bring it in. That town was a mess with lots of unemployment and many buildings boarded up.

I called the tax office in Atlantic City and inquired as to whether there were any upcoming auctions of any properties. As it turned out, there were to be some soon.

It was music to my ears.

The fellow I talked to sounded very nice and efficient. I asked if he could put together a list of for me, and he did, including the opening bid prices.

I went down by myself, but I told Bud I was going. I had just bought three lots in New York at auction, two in Harlem and one in the Bronx. I paid $300 each for the two in Manhattan and $450 for one in the Bronx. When I did that, he thought I was crazy. It was when the city was broke, and they were just trying to bring in taxes. This was the '70s. There were great bargains, but everyone there treated the lots as if they were dumping grounds.

The city would pick up the junk, including cars, and send a bill. It wasn't such a good deal anymore, so I sold for a profit and got out. Guess you know what happened a few years later—the prices went sky high. Oh well. It was fun.

So I made an appointment with the man in the tax office, and down I went to Atlantic City. I could not believe how many lots and buildings he had. They started at $300 and up, but not by much. I spent most of a day looking and writing down which lots I would bid on. He drove me and was not in a rush, which told me there was not much interest.

There were several lots on the water that I was interested in. One was a brick apartment building in the block just off the water, and it was in pristine condition. It was five stories with twelve apartments—opening bid: $9,000.

This was very exciting to me, and I asked Bud if he would go down with me for this sale. He remarked, "Don't you have enough poverty property?" I had not sold the others at that time.

He said yes but that he would invite our friends to go along, and we would have lunch in a great restaurant on the way.

We went into the building where the auction was being held. Not many people were there, and some must have been people losing property for the taxes. Bidding was fast. I really had my mind on that one building, but I bid on a couple of pieces, because they were going for nothing. But now my group thought it was funny, and they were even pulling my arm down.

I waited until the building came up, and I started bidding. Everyone in my group got up to leave because they could no longer contain their giggles.

I got distracted and missed my bids, so I got up to leave. Only one woman was bidding against me, and she got it for $12,500. I was shocked, but I had distraction, and it played to her advantage.

She could not believe she had gotten it. She asked the auctioneer, "Did I get it for $12,500?"

He said, "Yes, you did." I stood and watched her cry. Gambling came in a few months later.

I had my list for many years. Bud and Jack always admitted when we were all down gambling and having fun that they should have been bidding instead of laughing. I agreed.

Later on, in what I call our gambling days, Bud, Denise, and I made a quick getaway to Atlantic City. It was fun, and we stayed at the first hotel that opened with a casino—Resorts International. It had been called Haddon Hall back in the '20s. Denise and Louie had stayed there when they got married, so she was so excited to be going down. That night, we went down to dinner in the main dining room, and she was amazed that they had done nothing to the room. It was as she remembered all those years earlier. She kept looking up to the ceiling, which was beautiful with carvings. She told how they went by railroad on their honeymoon. Of course, back then, there were no planes as we know today, so the train was a big trip, and she said it was very elegant. It made her very happy to reminisce about such a happy time in her life.

Now another scene of abuse occurred, this time in front of our apartment building. A young man was literally pulling a young lady down the sidewalk with his arm around her neck and her feet barely touching the ground.

I ran into the Chinese restaurant next door and asked them to call the police and tell them what was happening. They said they would not get involved. I ran then to my doorman, but he did not have a phone. This was before cell phones. So I ran to the corner and used the pay phone. I called 911 and was connected to the seventeenth precinct and told them where to come.

By the time they arrived, which was very quickly, the man and woman were down the next block between Third and Second. I directed them down there. Of course, I went down to see how it would end.

The police officers jumped out of their vehicle, and another police car arrived. When they started trying to get her loose, the young man finally let her go, but he fought them, and it took about five of them to get him to the side of the police car. He knocked off their hats and one's eyeglasses. He spread-eagled on them. They finally used their billy clubs on the back of his legs to get him into the police car. They took her with them to press charges.

The next day, I went to the station to see what happened to the young lady. They told me she refused to press charges, so they had to let him go. She was another one who knew he would get out someday and come after her; it sure could not be she loved him.

Billy clubs did a terrific job, and I believe men would

actually be more afraid of walking around with no kneecaps than to have a gun held on them but not used. I keep one in my car in case of accident and doors will not open, and I can break a window with it or use it for a weapon if needed. I also keep one by my apartment door. Both are antiques.

The Salbs' son Scott came home after sailing from California to Australia, where he spent six months working. He was handsome and had lots of stories. Every girl wanted to go out with him, and some of the parents were interested in that happening too. He had gone out with some local girls a couple of times, but none more than once or twice.

He met Mary when the local teenagers had a bonfire on the beach, as it was an annual Fourth of July event. It lasted all night, and all the parents were okay with it, as they were all neighbors just having fun. He and Mary came walking up our driveway early in the morning. We could hear them all night long on the beach, so I was not worried about her. She was meeting a lot of the local young people for the first time.

We, of course, went to North Haven for all weekends, and she always went with us. So she and Scott spent every weekend partying with all the people their age. Scott worked at Baron's Cove Restaurant for some time and then moved to the city. Now they spent every night together.

This was very shortly after Mary came to New York. Scott was showing her great times, and I never worried about him not treating in a proper way with love and respect. She had always loved to swim, and to be on the boat with him meant many great weekends for her.

Frank Sinatra had his own table at Jilly's, and one night, he came in with about six people, including Barbara Marx. No one could ever just walk to the table. Mary was with us; we were celebrating her eighteenth birthday. Mary always loved his music, and she was so excited to even be in the same room with him.

Bud asked Sam if he could take Mary over to meet him. Sam first asked Frank and was given the okay. Sam took her, and she was introduced with the tears on her cheeks. Barbara very acidly said, "Oh, for God's sake, cut the tears."

Mary was mortified. Evidently, Barbara was insecure at that point, but Mary was just overwhelmed with meeting him.

When she got back to the bar and Bud heard the story, he said, "Well, you got to meet him; she cannot not take that away."

I was so happy for her, as she was now enjoying life so much, and she truly was maturing into a beautiful young woman. They had so much fun, and Scott took her everywhere. She was enjoying so many new things, and it reminded me of how Bud had showed me exciting venues I did not know existed.

They continued to date for a few years, and they made a great-looking couple.

Then he was transferred on his job to Illinois. She came to me, and she was very upset and told me although she did not believe in living with someone without being married, she wanted to go there with him. She said, "If I do not, he will meet someone else, and I will always regret not going, and he wants me to."

What could I say except to tell her to go? I knew she would be devastated if I did not. He made her happy, and that was all I wanted for her.

Then, after about a year, a call came, and they were going to get married. I was very happy. It meant stability for her, and they made a good couple.

Vicki had already married a local from Southampton. Bud and I were not happy with him. He turned out to be an alcoholic and an abuser after a child, Jason, was born. She eventually left him, but not until after Mary was married to Scott.

There was lots of planning for Scott and Mary's wedding. She and I were talking every day about the wedding dress. She wanted me to pick out the bridesmaid dresses, as most of her attendants would be New Yorkers. I went to Saks and found some I thought she would really like. I sent pictures and swatch colors. She liked them. I got the sizes of the girls and ordered. They all came in for fittings, and it was a very exciting time for all of us.

They were in Chicago, but the in-laws, Bud, and I were planning like crazy. I had family coming from all over. Bud was so excited that Mary had asked him to give her away. They came to Sag Harbor to talk to the priest about the wedding. Scott was raised Catholic, so Mary had to become Catholic to be married in the Catholic Church, so she did it all, including the necessary studying.

The priest asked Mary who would be giving her away, and she said her stepfather was giving her away. The priest asked if he was Catholic. She said he was divorced and that the Catholic Church no longer recognized him as a member.

"Well," he said, "I cannot marry you, then, with him giving you away." Mary looked him straight in the eye and said, "Then I will not be married in your church." Scott's parents were big church members, so he had a problem.

He quickly said that he would perform the ceremony. Money usually prevailed in such situations.

Denise's big desire was to have a wedding reception at her house. Being on the waterfront in North Haven with seven and a half acres of landscaped land, it was perfect. She was thrilled when Mary asked if they could have it there. She told them yes, and of course Mary was so happy. None of her other five granddaughters wanted a wedding like that, but Mary and Scott did.

It was a beautiful wedding, and Mary was one of the most beautiful brides with her antique-looking dress. They had a big tent, and the weather was perfect. Bud was beaming when he walked her down the aisle. I was the proud mother, and Denise was in her glory; she finally got the wedding she wanted at her home.

All my family came from everywhere for the wedding. What fun. The morning of the wedding, it was raining, and someone said to me, "What a shame."

I laughed and said, "God is just watering the flowers and the lawn." Just before going to the church, the sun came out.

After the ceremony, everyone went back to our house. We had a big tent in the yard facing the water and our beach house. The Salb house was close by on the beach, as well.

Everyone was dancing under the tent, and Bud, Denise, and I were very happy with all our parts working out as planned. The table was round, and it was now playing out for all of us. Tom Alten, Mary's father, was out of the picture. Mary had her protector, and I had mine. All was well.

CHAPTER 9
New Endeavors and Intrigue

I decided it was time for me to get out of the perfume business, and I decided to start looking for something else I might be interested in. Sure enough, I found an ad in the *Wall Street Journal* that intrigued me. Now if this wasn't different for a woman—stripping and refinishing of furniture! I had loved stripping paint from chairs or whatever when I was a kid, stripping objects back to bare wood and then just adding a stain and oil finish.

I called and made an appointment. The man said it was something he did at night. It was his second job, and it had become too much for him.

I think one of Bud's greatest traits was he never questioned me on anything I wanted to do. I was very independent, and Bud was secure enough to let me be.

I drove out to Kearny, New Jersey, that night, and there was an old three-story brick building with a huge graveled parking lot at the end of the road before the swamps. I went in and was so enthralled, because as even as I child, I loved old furniture, old homes, and so on. Time had lost meaning to me. There were no cell phones then, and I had already left the place. I got home, and Bud was walking the floor, afraid something had happened to me. I was so sorry. Never again did he have to worry about me letting him know when I would be home.

I kept him up most of the night because I was so excited, and I bought the business two days later.

I fell in love with that building and spent many happy days there. I do not know why I love antiques and old buildings so much, but I loved restoring them. I also live in an apartment building that was built in the 1920s even though I could live in any number of new apartment buildings in my neighborhood.

I worked hard as I did on the farm, but I loved it. I named my new business "Unfinished Business." It takes great patience to do that kind of labor, but I never tired of it. It grew fast. I hired high school boys to help me, and they were good. They were such gentlemen, and they had a hard time accepting the fact that I could lift as much as they could. I had to make them understand that they shouldn't stop what they were doing to help me. I appreciated it, but it was my way. I have never been weak, even at one hundred pounds.

I could hardly keep up with all the work. I closed down

the tanks where the previous owner dipped everything with strong chemicals. They destroyed the grain of the wood. Also, because the pieces had to be left in the tanks for a couple of days, many of them ended up warping.

I loved that place, but the young men thought I should have a dog, as it was really away from anything other than a box factory across the street. I did not worry, but they took me to the pound to look. I always laughed about it later. I did not pick out the dog; *she* picked *me*. We walked through, and I was really not interested, but at the last cage was a German shepherd named Missy. She pressed her head to the bars, and the woman from the pound said, "That's a first time she has ever made a move to anyone."

I said, "I am scared to death of big dogs."

Missy whined, and I walked over to pet her. I felt sorry for her. They took her out of the cage. She came to me but not the others. I was told that she had been trained no doubt as a guard dog but had been abused. These were key words for me to hear. No animal should be mistreated any more than a human being.

Missy had been picked up in the swamps, and she had cuts on her, and her neck was badly scarred from a collar she was wearing, as it was too small. I said, "I will try her; I am not sure I can handle her." I had raised toy poodles that weighed about three pounds each.

That dog was like a shadow to me. Anytime a man came to the door, she would place herself between me and the man, not menacingly but protectively.

Bud was happy with that. He came out one day, and we were having a sandwich. I put one half of mine down, and I told Bud that he could have it, because I was full. When he took it from the plate, Missy put her mouth around his wrist—not biting, just holding. I had to tell her it was okay, and then she released his wrist. Bud loved dogs, but he turned white on that one.

Another time, a man came to the door and said he was lost and asked me if I knew some company I did not know. He had a chain in his hand. He was standing on a three-step landing. Missy took one look at that chain and pushed him off that landing and spread-eagled over him. The poor man was scared to death, saying, "Please call her off!"

I was down the steps in two seconds, and I said, "Missy, it is okay." She jumped right off. That scared me too. I said to the man, "She is a trained guard dog, and the chain in your hand spooked her." I apologized to him. I may have been mistaken to apologize, as when I now think back, why was he carrying a heavy chain? Maybe to rob me or even worse.

Another time was so very funny the way it ended. I got a call from the Kearny, New Jersey, police department late one night to tell me that they'd had a call from the neighbors of my building who had heard a big commotion in my huge yard—someone running and Missy barking. When they got there, Missy was sitting at an open window. They had called Frank, a young man who lived in Kearny and worked for me. He was on his way, as he was on the list at the police department in case of an emergency.

They said, "We think everything is okay. She is now at the front door. We hear her sniffing, but we are not going in till your employee gets here."

Frank arrived, and everything was in order except for the open window in the back. I will bet that guy never tried to go in a window in a desolate area again. I kind of wished Missy had let him in and then gotten him. It might have been a big mess, though.

I had met a man named Merve Bendewald, who was a good ol' cowboy from Montana. He had come to live in New York after graduating college, although he loved his background. He was a lot like me; he was also from a big family. He knew he did not want to be a rancher. He had gotten a good education and left with his cowboy boots to go to the Big Apple.

He moved in to the Y and then to Hudson and Tenth. He was the most creative person I have ever known. He could make a collector's piece out of what was called trash or junk. Merve wanted to expand his life, and did he ever! He had a shop on Hudson and Tenth called the Village Stripper. He was commonly known as "the mayor of Hudson Street."

He was doing stripping of furniture but hated it. It is very dirty work, and he did not have the space to do it. He asked me if I would pick up the items and do the labor. I would collect and just pay him a nominal finder's fee. The people would drop things off at his shop, and then I would pick them up and take them to my shop. That way, they would still come in and buy antiques from him, which was his main business. I said okay. We did this for some time, and it was a good relationship.

One day, I got a call to the Upper West Side. I made the estimate, and the gentleman—who happened to be the general manager of one of our prestigious entertainment businesses—asked if I was driving back though midtown. He was late to get to his office. I said yes and that I would be happy to drop him off.

We were riding down, and I had one of Bud's business cards lying in the ashtray. He said, "Nadine, how do you know Bud Schramm?"

I am a jokester, so I laughed and said, "I sleep with him."

He then realized that I was Bud's wife. He said, "Can I call Bud and kid him?"

I said, "Sure."

He called Bud and told him he just met a woman who said she slept with him. It took Bud a minute, and then his remark was that I had "pulled another funny."

That reminds me of another fun evening with Bud. We were invited to a party at a restaurant, Maria's Cin Cin, where we ate fairly often. It was owned by a couple—Brag Bragalini, the chef, and his wife, Maria. It was at 224 East Fifty-Third in New York City. It was a very popular hangout for the advertising industry. It was called the purple martini party. We went, and I met a young man about twenty-five years old. He had already had a couple of the purple martinis. Bud had walked away to talk to someone he knew. This young man was writing a story for the *Wall Street Journal*. He asked me what I did, and I told him I was a stripper. I knew this was going to be fun, but come on, I was a furniture stripper.

Well, this poor kid said, "Well, where do you strip?"

I said, "New Jersey."

The joke was going perfectly up to that point.

"Where do you work? Do you have a card with the address?"

I said, "No, but my husband does. I will give it to you later."

He asked, "Does it bother your husband what you do?"

I said, "No, I make good money, but it is hard work."

Bud walked up, and I introduced him. I pulled out my card and gave it to the young man. He looked and said, "Oh my God, you fooled me." He said to Bud, "Well, she is gorgeous enough to be a stripper." He left shortly after.

He did not have a story in the *Wall Street Journal*, but I bet he had a massive hangover. Bud never knew what to expect of me, but he told the story to all his friends.

One building I enjoyed so much was the old John Jacob Astor countinghouse. It is at 21 West Twenty-Sixth Street. It was where Mr. Astor collected rents from tenement buildings all along the streets on the West Side. John Jacob owned many buildings. Today he would be called a slumlord, but it was very much needed housing at the time. Perhaps even Mr. Schramm Sr. lived there when he arrived as a sixteen-year-old with no money. That would be ironic as you will see when you finish my story.

A literary agent had bought the building and called me to restore all the woodwork. I went in the evening to look at it and give an estimate. The problem, though, was I could not see except with a flashlight. Oh my, was I excited. I knew from looking at it that underneath all the thirty to forty coats of paint it was beautiful walnut wood.

I had a group of young people working for me. We stripped paint off the mantels, doors, moldings, and the ceilings, which were very high in the entrance. We lay on scaffolding to remove paint from the vestibule, which was heavily carved, using toothbrushes, dentist tools, and anything else we could think of. It was tedious work, but we all loved the results. Each one could only lie on his or her back for a short time and then crawl down and another go up for a turn. It was one of the more tedious jobs but also the most rewarding.

The original huge vault was still there. It must have weighed tons. It had a huge red rose painted on the door. It was never changed in all those years. I went back to see it in the last few years and was so happy to see that nothing had been painted over it. It is beautiful, and I am so glad to have had the opportunity to leave my mark there. I never overcharged. In fact, I should have charged more and paid my workers a higher salary. But I enjoyed the work so much that it did not enter my mind.

When Mr. Astor owned it, the tenants paid their monthly or weekly rent just as if they were making a deposit in a bank through brass dividers to the tellers. That portion had never been painted. We just polished it up.

The wife of the man who hired me researched and found copies of wallpaper of that era. It really turned out so well. This was a period when many people were buying up apartments and bringing them back to the original natural wood.

I did work for lots of interesting people. One was Lorne Michaels, producer of *Saturday Night Live.* It was his first year of the show, which has become one of the longest running. My company Budd Enterprises has delivered items to the set for years. At that time, I would never have dreamed of that happening.

He bought this wonderful apartment on Central Park West. All the woodwork was painted over. My crew and I worked there for several weeks. He was the easiest to work for. He worked until late every night. We arrived early every morning to start our work.

The first thing I did every morning was clean up the kitchen. He evidently loved Chinese carryout food then. Since we would need the sink for our washup, it made sense for me to clean up a little.

I saw very little of him. He just told me what he wanted and did not worry. The only thing I remember him having us change was the color of the stain for the woodwork. I am sure he must be very easy to work with on the show.

I also did work for Glenn Close when she was young. She had an apartment down in the West 20s. I remember a piece I stripped, stained, and put an oil finish on. It was a folding step stool. It was out of alignment, and I do not think I ever got it straightened out. I did some other things in the apartment too.

She was a very nice young person. I was always happy that she became a star.

I have a huge oak mantel in our living room that I took from a house that was being torn down in Rutherford, New Jersey. It was so heavily painted that quarter-inch grooves were completely filled with paint. I just set it over in the corner of the workshop, and I would walk over and work on it a little at a time from the jobs we were doing. Bud thought it was going to be too big for our fireplace, but I showed how it would fit. He put it in, and we loved it.

I made another great find on the street. I was driving across town to the Lincoln Tunnel one morning at about 6:00 a.m. I saw an oak five-drawer filing cabinet sitting out as garbage. Now, to me, something like that should never go to the junkyard. I could manage very heavy pieces, but that was more than I could do alone. I saw a young man coming down the sidewalk, and I said to him, "How would you like to make a quick five dollars?"

He said with an almost scared look, "What do I have to do?"

I said, "Help me load this in."

He did, and I felt great about saving something someone else could enjoy for years to come. It is, of course, now a collector's item. Just remembering all the work and then seeing the beauty makes me happy.

All doors in our apartment were also a mess. I also refinished them and just stained and oiled them. They belong in our building, which was built in the late 1920s. When I look at them, I wonder how in the world I did all that heavy work, but now I know it was just out of love for the beauty of the old. It had become a rage to save doors in the city, and we must have done at least five hundred.

I had a big station wagon, but I decided I needed a truck to pick up all the work. I bought a used US mail truck with sliding doors on either side. I have always worn heels and did every day. I kept the doors open, as of course there was no air-conditioning. I was on the Jersey Turnpike every day.

I was laughing one day to Bud about big-rig drivers who would pull alongside and give me thumbs-up. A woman driving a truck was unusual back then. Today, women drive trailer rigs. Bud said, "You are going to cause accidents. You'd better close those doors."

I only had one job that was a disappointment—not in the work but of the man who contracted me. I had to remove the paint off old wooden shutters for him. I had done many before, but it was really tedious. We did all twenty of them, and I delivered them. The man said, "You did not do a good job." I looked at him in disbelief. He lived between the river and the West End. I wish I remembered his name;

I would put it here. He handed me a check for half the price that we had agreed on. I had already unloaded them. I just drove away, but I was mad. I had paid more in labor than I got from him. Well, you run into a jerk every once in a while in any business. He was rated as a triple jerk in my mind. I never took another job of shutters.

I did the work for about five years, and Bud began to see me working much too hard, lifting doors or furniture that was very heavy. He knew I loved it, but he thought it was taking a toll on my health. He was right. He told me to just do some for fun, so I sold the business to a man. I do not think he kept it long. It was really hard work, and you had to love it or you would soon tire of it.

I knew I still had a lot of unfinished business, so my mind was on opening something new. I will never think I am finished, I guess. I cannot sit still. I have to be on the go. I do not know what people do when they get up in the morning and have no schedule to fulfill. I have a saying: "Better to wear out than to rust out." I live by it.

Merve Bendewald asked me to come into business with him selling antiques at the Village Stripper, but when the owner of the building tripled the lease for Village Stripper, we decided we would close the store. We had done enough.

Merve and I were both at loose ends. He called and asked me to come down for lunch because he had something he would like me to help him with. I went down, and he started telling me about this jewelry from South Dakota that he had always loved—Landstrom's Black Hills Gold. He has been asked to come out to think about bringing the line to New York, and he said, "I want you to do this with me."

I said, "Merve, what is the deal?" He explained that we would fly out there, and they were having a golf tournament—all expenses paid. I had become a golfer, and so was he. I said, "Let me talk to Bud about this."

I told Bud, and he said, "Let's see. In my mind, there is no losing on this offer. You go play a round of golf, and if you do not like the deal, you have lost nothing."

We went to Rapid City, but it was 1:00 p.m. when we got there, and we had not eaten. I could not play a round of golf without food. I ran and asked the clubhouse personnel to make quick sandwiches for us.

All the players were ready to go. We walked out, and introductions were made. I was to play with the CEO, Chuck Dages.

Another Capricorn day for me, I thought. But I like my sign; it is a goat who can climb mountains.

Chuck was a tall, athletic man. *Stay steady*, I thought. He gave me honors, and I hit a decent ball. He hit, and I said, "Boy, I think I am going to have my hands full." I relaxed and said to myself, "Have a good time; you are on a mini-vacation." We started talking and laughing, and I really got into my game. We ended up with both having a good game as well as the others playing with us.

Later, there was a dinner, and Merve and I were introduced.

Chuck said, "Merve and Nadine are here from New York, and we are trying to get them to represent us in the Northeast. I will tell you if Nadine can sell jewelry like she plays golf, we will have to increase production."

It did not take Merve long to know he did not enjoy or want to sell jewelry. I could not sell the Black Hills in New York. New Yorkers want mostly 18-, 20-, or 24-karat gold. This was 10-, 12-, or 14-karat gold. I was sorry I could not sell it because all the people who worked there were so nice. Also, the jewelry was quiet attractive.

At that meeting, I met other jewelry salespeople, and one asked me to represent Designs by the Sea, a company she was working with in Texas. They needed someone in the New York area. The sales manager flew to New York to meet me and acquaint me with the line. I fell in love with it. It was semiprecious stones with gold filigree.

The way I became a golfer is good for a laugh for all golfers. Bud said to me one day, "How would you like to play golf?" Well, I had always been athletic, so I was all for it. He had played when younger but had to give it up with family and business being very demanding.

I got ten lessons with Richard Metz, a top teacher, for Christmas from Bud. I was very excited to learn something new that we could share. I had to buy golf shoes.

Now I have laughed many times over this. I wore nothing except high heels, and of course, they were showing me golf shoes. I tried a few pairs on, and I was not comfortable in low heels. I said to the guy, "Do you have any with higher heels?" He did not laugh, but I bet he told the story more than a few times. He told me that I would get used to them.

Well, I got used to the shoes, and I loved golf. Now I had found my new position to be much fun, and I also enjoyed meeting so many jewelers. I really liked selling the jewelry and was very successful. In a very short time, they had a competition for salespeople. The winner would have a week in Hawaii, all expenses paid.

Bud said, "Well, can you go somewhere else if you win?" We had been there many times. I told him, "Listen, I just started; I am not going to win."

I got in the race, and it was nip and tuck daily between a gentleman from California who had been selling for twenty years and me. Every day, they gave us a total from the main office. Bud asked me each day how much I had sold. I laughed because he was more into it than I was.

I won.

We went to Hawaii and had a great time. We took extra time on our own and at our expense. After all, the airfare was paid, so we were on a very inexpensive trip. I ended up representing five companies. I covered New York, New Jersey, Connecticut, and the Virgin Islands.

I loved working with the owners of Designs by the Sea, especially George Kalergis. We could sell more than all the booths at jewelry shows around us. We both loved what we did. We were laughing while others around us were uptight about sales.

I had accounts when Bud passed away. I gave them up to run Budd Enterprises. The largest one was Fortunoff's, but I also handled many other chains, and then all the small mom-and-pop stores, and I loved my customers and always wanted to give them what I thought would sell for them. I also wanted to know about their kids and family. Sales are great, but there is much more to life. You never know how each person will affect you.

I knew we could be good partners, as we had done so much business together already just with the stripping business. I loved furniture and antiques, but I did not know enough to be on the selling side. I had started buying and selling from my shop in New Jersey, but more to just help people who were moving to smaller homes or selling for need of money.

I had trouble sometimes, as I saw people giving up items I knew had been a great part of their lives. They usually had children who did not want to take any of it. One house I walked into had beautiful silver, china, and furniture. They were moving into a trailer home to make their life easier. In all probability, it was to raise money, so I suggested they keep the silverware and some other items that would not take up much space. I told them the children would regret it later on if many of the items were sold; they were just too young to realize it now.

But the couple said that they had asked them more than once, so I bought everything. I found this to be the easy way rather than have others dealers come in and pick the good and leave them with having to get rid of junk or take it to the dump.

That happened to me several times. I would always keep one or two items so I would remember them. They had to have some heartbreak with giving up their homes.

Ralph was named president of the Senior Democratic Party of Arkansas by Dale Bumpers. He loved it. He had no desire to be a politician, but he sure enjoyed helping others who he thought would do a good job for the people of Arkansas or nationally. He also was named as a judge to the racetrack in Hot Springs, Arkansas, as well as the state parole board.

We were once having our family reunion in Hot Springs when Ralph was a judge at the racetrack. We all went, and we had box seats thanks to him. We were placing our bets and laughing about who won and who lost. I love to gamble a bit, so I always bet a long shot on every race. I bet on a horse that evidently no one else thought could possibly win. The horse came in, and I was the big winner, but there was not much money on it.

Ralph came down to see us, and the big talk was about Nadine's long-shot win. Ralph said, "Why did you not tell us about this horse? What did you know?"

I said, "Nothing, but hey, you're the one sitting up there. Do you have any tips for us?"

Before Jimmy Carter ran for the presidency, the Democratic Party wanted Dale Bumpers to run for the presidency. He had gone back to Arkansas to talk to six of his friends he respected, my brother included, and he decided not to run. The convention was held in New York, and Jimmy Carter was chosen.

Dale called me to come over to visit in his suite at the Waldorf. We caught up on a lot of family and Arkansas news, and I asked him why he would not accept. I told him that I thought he would make a great president. He said it was not worth it to put his family through the process.

He said, "Call Bud and have him come over. We will

meet downstairs at the Bull and Bear for lunch." Bud met us at the door, but there were no seats.

Well, the newspaper owner for the *Arkansas Democrat-Gazette* was there, so Dale asked him, "Do you have any pull?"

They walked us to the table with Dale being introduced as the senator from Arkansas. Well, they made a mistake and thought Bud was the senator and kept addressing him as such. Dale laughed and said, "So be senator for a day."

Bud said later, "I am probably the only senator who ever paid for lunch."

Although Chelsea Warehouses was large, it began to have problems with cash flow. New York City was in a terrible mess. Taxes were raised on all real estate.

We had seven warehouses and were getting returns of 1 percent.

There was no way you could run a business with that kind of return.

Bud tried to get his uncle to step down as president so decisions could be made to reorganize. His uncle only came in to see what checks came in, and then he would leave to play golf or, in the wintertime, head to Florida. He was a very nice man, but he had no business sense.

Bud had never worked for anyone else—just the family

business. I knew it would be very hard for him to have a person make decisions for him.

The time had come when Chelsea was in negotiation for sale with another Allied agent, Morgan Manhattan. I filed papers with the State of Delaware for a business. I did not tell Bud, but I knew he would need to do something.

I filed papers as corporation and named it Budd Enterprises Ltd. Bud was his nickname, but the extra *d* made it look a little more professional and still covered his name.

I covered everything I could think of—real estate and so on—but knew trucking should be the main business. That was 1979.

I had my business, and every morning, I went to my bank to make deposits. The bank was Manufacturers Hanover at Forty-Sixth and Lexington Avenue. Women business owners were rare, and it was interesting to me that I was the only one at that bank. The other thing was the manager was a woman, which was also rare.

The manager called me to her desk almost every day to have a coffee with her. I was always in a rush, but she really wanted to know all about my business. She asked me what my husband did, and I told her. I also told her that the company was in negotiations to sell.

When the business was sold, Bud was requested to go

with the buyers. The buyers did not know anything about the television business or how to run transportation for the Macy's Thanksgiving Day Parade. Also, the concerts in the parks for the Metropolitan Opera and the New York Philharmonic were also part of why they needed him. He was the one who had started that portion of business for Chelsea.

I pushed Bud terribly hard for several months to go and ask if they would sell him back that portion. He thought it would be unethical. I said, "No, they bought you for the seven warehouse buildings and the property. You are a now a free agent."

It took quite a lot of talk from me, but he did take my advice and was so happy. He did not to have to deal with family issues anymore. The theatrical industry only dealt with him.

Rick Schramm was the only one who was still young and had been brought into the business. Ray Schramm gave him peanuts for salary. He had served in the marines. I am sure Rick was excited to be going into the family business that his dad had worked in and died when he was very young. When the business was sold, Rick went to a moving company in New Jersey and worked there for some number of years.

Well, now I also knew Bud was thinking of the money he would need if he tried to buy the company back, but now I was having talks with my banker. I told her about the contracts and the business. She said if he has those contracts, the bank would arrange any money he needed. Contracts were the same as money in the bank with corporations like those.

I made him read a book called *Those Fabulous Greeks* on Aristotle Onassis and his brother-in-law Stavros Niarchos. They had bought tanker ships from the US federal government that were rusting out after being stored on the river since World War II. They had paid almost nothing and had gotten contracts from the oil companies to haul oil with very little money down. Who else would think of a way to use them? They were actually just parked in the East River rusting out. That is how they made their huge amounts of money. The world did not know so much about it until he married Jackie Kennedy.

Well, Bud did read it but was still reluctant, so one morning, I told a little lie. I said I needed him to go to my bank with me. Of course, I had it set up to have my coffee with the bank manager as usual. Bud, always the gentleman, thought nothing of being asked to sit with us. The manager immediately asked what he did, and he told her that the company had been sold and so on.

She said, "Now wait a minute. You are working for someone else for the first time in your life?"

Bud said yes.

She said, "Well, I guess you have a secure job, since it seems that you are the only one with the knowledge about the theatrical industry."

He said, "Yes, that is true, and they do not seem to want to know about it."

Well, he walked right into this conversation not knowing two women were plotting for a big change in his life.

I said, "Listen, I have an appointment, and I have to leave, so you two finish up your coffee."

That night, he told me, "I cannot believe she would raise the money if I wanted to go on my own."

I was so happy he had talked to her, and I said, "I think she is right." I only occasionally mentioned it, waiting for the outcome.

One night, he said, "You are not going to believe what happened today."

I was thinking, *Oh boy! Maybe?* I asked, "What?"

He said, "I went today and asked Sadler Morgan about the contracts to see if it was possible to maybe make a deal." He had made us our usual cocktails, and he was smiling ear to ear.

I laughed and said, "And what was the answer?"

"He said, 'Bud, that business belongs to you, so take

it. We bought yours for the warehouses.' Nadine, you were right. How did you know?"

I replied, "You were standing too close to the trees, as the old saying goes." I then asked how much they wanted for it.

He said, "They answered, 'Nothing. You were the one who brought it into Chelsea. The customers never wanted to talk to anyone but you, so you deserve it. Our family has known your family for a hundred years, and you have carried the burden for all the years after your father died.'"

Then I said, "Well, I will be right back." I went into my office, pulled out my folder with the corporation papers, and handed it to him.

He looked at it and said, "My God. You did this a year ago when we were just working on the sale."

Yes. We needed to be prepared for change.

I said, "One thing has to be changed."

He asked, "What?"

I said, "I had to make myself president to file the papers, so now you become president, and I am vice president."

Now the big thing to him was to meet the customers and see if they would go with him in the new company—Budd Enterprises Ltd.

They all said, "Bud, we do not even know those other

people. We've always dealt with you. Of course it is yours. Get the paperwork for us."

Then it was off to the banker. She just asked, "How much do you need?"

Bud had it all figured out. He would lease equipment and buy as he made profits.

She said, "But you need money to start."

He finally financed one van with her. He ended up buying seven trucks used at CBS and Carroll Music, renters of musical instruments. All equipment was leased for the other parts, such as the Macy's Thanksgiving Day Parade, the Metropolitan Opera concerts, and the New York Philharmonic Concerts in the Park.

Dennis Curry, who had worked at CBS, and Bud had become close friends. They remained so when Dennis became partner at Carroll Music, and they had lunch together every week. Dennis even took me or I took him for several years after Bud passed away.

While Dennis was still at CBS, they had done the 1968 conventions together. Bud was still at Chelsea, and Dennis was head of the transportation for the network. It was quite different then for transportation needs for the conventions from what it is today—eighteen trailer loads of cables, cameras, and other equipment, which were heavy loads and also very expensive.

Republicans were in Florida, and Democrats were in Chicago, three days apart. It was really hot in Florida, and of course, they were working outside. It was a real push to get everything loaded and to Chicago on time. Also, there was the problem with the rioters in Chicago.

Bud had the FBI sticker on his briefcase when he came home. He was not sure if it made him a target, but nothing happened. It was really a bad scene. He ended up with complete exhaustion from the whole thing. He went to the doctors and was told to rest up.

Bud's father brought him in at around age twelve, having him pick up suitcases for storage in the warehouses. So I knew Bud would be successful in his new business. He had done it all. He was so happy not meeting with partners who agreed on very little and all the pressure on him to bring in the larger part of business and then watch it go out the door in the wrong directions. With him, the money was spent wisely, and profits were his.

By the time Bud was twenty-two, his father had put him in charge of a huge move by one of the top oil companies to California. It took six months to move it all. Bud came up with the idea of moving the executives in an unusual way at the time. He shipped by plane the most important items so that they could move into a house instead of having to stay in a hotel.

This was major in those years when it took so long to move cross country, not like today with all the major highways. Most roads at that time were two lanes like Route 66.

He also told me the ratio of women to men in California was six to one. He said he got so many invitations from women who just happened to have seats to events very often.

Later, he tried to get Governor Rockefeller to let truckers use tandem trailers, but he was thirty years ahead of time. There were pictures of Bud with Lieutenant Governor Malcolm Wilson making the request. He had on a big black hat, trying to look older than his thirty years or so. Instead, I am afraid he looked Mafia. He told them it would save fuel and wear on the roads, but it was to no avail. Today, it is common to see them. Too bad they did not listen to him. It saves tremendous cost to truckers and in turns saves on the cost of all goods. Bud was always a visionary.

CHAPTER 10

One Happy Grandma

I had gotten a call to come to Illinois when my grandson John Michael was born in April 1981.

John Michael was a preemie and weighed three pounds four ounces, so needless to say, I was worried about Mary and Scott as well as the baby. I knew they would need help when the doctors decided he should go home instead of holding him in the hospital. All his vital signs were very strong, and they thought he would be better off without being subjected to germs from others. They usually keep preemies until they weigh five or six pounds.

I asked Mary and Scott if they would like for me to come to help out, and they were very happy to have me. Scott is very tall, and I remember him holding his tiny son in his large hand. He only came maybe three inches above Scott's wrist.

An issue was finding clothing to fit. A month or so before, I read an article in *Family Circle* of a young woman who had a preemie in Wisconsin, and after not being able to get clothing for her child that fit, she had started a company making preemie clothes. I still had the magazine article, so I called her.

She said, "I am so overbooked. I do not think I can help."

I said, "Please, just one piece."

She did send one to Mary so she could take him home from the hospital in a piece of clothing that fit. It meant so much to them.

I drove out in my big SUV loaded with everything they needed, including a baby bed, rocker, and anything I could think of that they would need. We had talked of my bringing those things out beforehand.

I was one happy grandmother, but I must say when I saw him, it was quite a shock to see one so small, but he was mighty and very strong for such a little one. He gained weight and grew, and the doctors told them he would catch up but not until he was going to school. He was growing and learning in every way as any child does; he was just smaller. Today, you would never know he was a preemie. In every other way, he was very normal.

As I was driving back from Chicago, Merve called Bud and said, "Tell Nadine I need to get together with her tonight. Meet us at the Grifone restaurant at 224 East Forty-Sixth Street at 8:00 p.m."

Bud called me on my CB, which I had bought for the trip, as he had insisted on my having it while driving to Chicago by myself. I was so glad I had bought it for the trip, as it was great company just listening to all the truckers talking to each other. Just hearing their stories keep me alert.

Bud told me we were to meet Merve and Judy, his wife. I said, "Bud I have been driving all day. Not tonight."

Bud said, "He really sounded like it was really important."

I said okay.

I got home, and we went for the meeting at the Grifone. Merve and Judy were sitting at the bar. We ordered drinks, and before the drinks even arrived, Merve pulled out a sock tied at the top, threw it on the bar in front of me, and said, "Open it." I did, and out came a mess of stuff—a gold watch, gold coins, and other items.

I look at the items and asked, "What are you showing these to me for?"

He said, "Remember that metal table and chairs we bought? Well, when I got it open, I found all of this. We will just divide it up."

We did. He wanted the watch, so I took the coins.

I told him, "You are a great partner. You could have taken it all."

He said, "No, I could not—the same as you."

He was right.

I was so happy to be a grandmother. Mary and Scott moved to Connecticut within the year. Mary would let me bring Michael into the city for a couple of days at a time when he was a few months old.

Mary has shared all her children with me. Amanda Dianne was the second, and then came Kelly Nadine. I was lucky I was a grandmother who wanted to babysit, and the other did not. Well, those bonding years have worked very well for us. I got to spend time with them.

A funny thing had happened. Scott and Mary agreed they would not name their children after their parents. Now Mary felt I had done so much at Michael's birth that I deserved to have one named after me, so she played with the alphabet, mixed up the letters in my name, and came up with Amanda Dianne.

Scott did not pick up on it and liked the name. Now Kelly was born, and they did the exact same, but this time Scott told her, "Listen, your mother has been such a good grandmother. I would like to break our agreement and name the third one after her."

Mary, of course, said it was a great idea. But this time, it was plainly Kelly Nadine without the trouble of playing with the letters.

I loved having the grandchildren in as soon as they were old enough to come in. Mike was never afraid to just get on trains by the age of eight, as he had a huge fascination for them. One trip I remember especially was a gift of me going up and taking him on a train ride from Stamford, where they lived, to New Haven and then getting on a train and coming back into Manhattan. I went up with him to the conductor and told him of Michael's love of trains.

Well, he told Michael all about trains and blew the whistle for him. I have never seen a child so thrilled. Then he let Michael pull the chain. You had to see the face of a child who had such a love, and then he got to actually ride with the conductor.

Saint Croix was always fun, but we did have one major problem. I was representing the jewelry manufacturers at the time, and I had to go to Saint Thomas to spend the day taking Christmas orders from the largest jewelers. They had so many stores there, as the cruise ships all stopped there. It was like a stampede with all the Americans rushing to the stores as if they were giving merchandise away.

Bud went along that time too and spent the day leisurely walking around and enjoying the local bars.

When I had finished, we grabbed the plane over to Saint Croix to spend a few days. There were only about four of us on this big plane. It was unusual, but I didn't think much of it. Now there had been a hurricane building up in the ocean.

We were landing and Bud said, "There's something wrong. There are no planes here except ones being worked on."

I said, "Bud, what happened to that storm Hugo that was a long way off a week ago?"

He said, "I have been so busy trying to get away I have paid no attention to it."

We got off. That plane had the steps up and took off so fast we had not even gotten inside the airport. Right away, he went over to ask what was going on in Saint Croix. They said they were getting ready for the hurricane. That was the last plane in or out. That was a major issue.

I know nothing about hurricanes, but Bud had seen damage on Long Island during one when his father's large motorboat was blown out of the water and destroyed. How we planned on handling the problem as it now approached the island was the issue.

It was an absolutely beautiful sunny day. How could something bad be so close to our island? We got up early the next morning, going to the hardware store to get supplies. Bud was not so worried at that point about food, but he wanted to get oil lamps, candles, tape, flashlights, an ax, a saw, and so on. This was serious stuff. Then it was on to get food supplies, bandages, and antiseptics. I said to myself, "He thinks this is going to be bad."

Bud stayed up the night before tracking the storm on television and maps. They were saying it was going to miss us.

He said, "No way. They are misreading charts and the island winds patterns."

Well, I did not say a word. I knew Bud knew how to read wind conditions, having flown his own plane and being an avid boatman.

We went back to the condo. I start taping windows in our condo. I sealed the plate-glass sliding doors, which were about twenty feet across in the living room and the bedroom combined. Then I crisscrossed tape every way.

I did not know what I was doing, but it worked. Next, I went out to the pool, and I threw all the pool furniture into the pool.

One lady came out and said, "What are you doing?"

I said, "I am not sure, but it makes sense to me so it will not be a projectile."

We had bought most of the tape the hardware store had. We knew we had to also try to help the ones who were not there. It was off season, so only the ones who lived year round were there except for a young pilot who rented one of the units with other ones in training.

The trainees got their credit by flying small planes in the Caribbean. He had an airline hostess visiting him. He had a bad ear infection and was afraid to fly out when he knew the storm would hit. If the eardrum burst, his career would end. It was not the group you would pick to share a disaster with.

There was a couple on the second floor, and the man was on oxygen and bedridden. Hazel, the wife of the manager, was there alone. Her husband had disappeared with a single owner a month before. There were two Arab couples with a couple of small children whom none of us ever saw. We saw only the men going to work or home for lunch.

We had insisted that the new manager and his wife, Tom and Sarah Dolan, come join us at Estate Carlton Condos. They had been hired by our association to take over in two weeks. They were living at the beach club that we all belonged to. They were in a small cottage on the water. We knew from the magnitude of the storm that it was not safe for them to stay there, and we knew we were going to need them. Thankfully, they listened to us.

We took full responsibility for their early employment by our group. I do not know what Bud and I would have done without them in the first forty-eight hours and the whole following time of rebuilding. We worked around the clock trying to bring some order to our plight.

Their cottage was destroyed and filled with sand. They might not have survived.

We called everyone together to prepare for the arrival of the winds and possible water surges, which are usually the killers in hurricanes. Bud told them he had been through a hurricane and it could be really bad. Maybe we would get lucky, but it didn't look good. He was sure we were going to take a direct hit.

He invited them to all come to our place, but all wanted to stay in theirs. The sick man could not be brought down, hospital bed and all.

The winds started to pick up at about 11:00 p.m. It was pitch black out. By midnight, Bud said, "Okay, we need to go into the hall that is away from the windows." It was now brutal.

We knew in many ways our building should stand, but we were not so sure of the roofs. It was Spanish style and had steel beams and one foot of concrete.

All of a sudden, we heard major noise, and water started pouring in down from the second floor into our hallway. Bud said the air conditioners had blown out. I grabbed about five towels and started mopping. I would wring them out into a bucket and hand the bucket to Bud. He would pour it down the bathtub. Then suddenly, the wind just quit.

Bud said, "Okay. We probably have a half hour or so before the second half comes." He had explained it to me before, so I knew what to expect.

We went out into a courtyard, and all the others come out. The first thing out of everyone's mouth was "Oh, my God. I am so glad it's over. I thought we were all going to die."

In a calm voice, Bud said, "We have a while, but then the second half will come over." He explained how the storm was a big circle, and in the center was called the eye. "There, it is still as a mouse."

Not a leaf was moving. The rain had stopped also. And he said it was quite possible the second half would be stronger.

It seemed like the storm stayed over the island forever.

One whole hour went by, and then it hit again, much stronger than before. Our nerves were shot, and we were filled with fear. I was exhausted, so I took a blanket and lay down on the tile floor in the hall at about 5:00 a.m. I actually fell asleep, but only for a few minutes. I jumped up saying how sorry I was for going to sleep.

We were waiting for the dawn to see the damage.

You could never imagine. There was not a leaf left on any tree or shrub. The grass was brown. Big trees had been uprooted.

Our building was cement, and the paint was off in strips a foot wide by five feet or more. Again, not a thing was moving. No birds were singing. Nothing. Then we heard all the natives nearby. They were already trying to get some things done, but there was no electricity or water.

Roofs were off. It turned out that about 80 percent of roofs were gone on the island.

The main road had all these huge, beautiful fifty- to seventy-five-year-old trees down and blocking the road completely. There was no power on the whole island, and these local men were out there with little handsaws trying to open the road.

We made sure we went through every condo to mop water and hang everything out over the balcony to dry. There were no telephones, and this was before cell phones.

No one came to the island to check. Saint Thomas and Puerto Rico had been hit, but not nearly like Saint Croix. At that time, we had no news, so we did not know where else it had hit. Our family was going crazy without contact.

We went to the airport. It was totally destroyed. The runway was covered with debris and sheet iron from the buildings and roofs. We were starting to conserve gas, as no stations are open. There was no electricity, and no gas pumps were working.

It was one big mess. We had the pilot and his girlfriend with us. We tried to clean the airport up, knowing we needed someone to land with so many needy people much worse off than we were. Good thing we did, because two days later, we saw a small plane fly in and circle, looking for a good landing space. It landed in the space we had cleared.

We jumped in our car and got out there. It was a crew with a newsman from CBS.

I said, "Please just call this number I have written down and let them know we are okay."

He said, "I have a very long list from Saint Thomas. I cannot promise."

I said, "Look, we do the trucking for CBS and have for years. Just say we are okay, no conversation."

He did make the call. I do not use an account for special favors. This time it was crucial to me. What a relief for family and friends when that call came in.

The next day, a huge US military cargo plane came in. Again, we ran but were not allowed near it, even with our young pilot with his credentials. But we saw them unloading heavy stuff. Then we found out they had set up tents in the field as headquarters. So Bud and I went to talk to the highest ranking in command.

We told them of our condo and that we had about forty units we could make available as their headquarters. Without electricity, we could not use them, but they would have the ability to bring in the power. Our sales ability worked, however, not until a few days after we came back to New York. They had to get clearance, no doubt. They moved in and stayed for several months, and they were armed. This was really very good, because there was lots of theft simply because so many had lost everything.

We used water from the pool to clean up a lot, chemicals and all. It was better than nothing, and there was a lot of mud everywhere from the heavy rains.

When that first big army plane came in, they gave everyone a chance to fly back to the States. Bud asked where they were landing, and they said Miami. Bud knew that Miami was likely in the path of the storm.

He said, "I am not going to take a chance on having to live through this one again."

If it was going to hit Miami, there would be no available seats to New York.

People were walking to the airport barefooted, feet bloodied from glass all over the roads, with ragged clothes and carrying kids sometimes.

They crawled on that plane. We were lucky we had a roof over our heads. It hit Charleston, South Carolina, at 140 miles an hour. The measurement in Saint Croix was 240 miles an hour, and that was when the measuring apparatus was blown to pieces.

In Saint Croix, there was no water surge, which is usually when there are lots of deaths. They said because the wind was so strong, it just flattened out the water.

Hugo was the name of the storm. It should have just been named Huge.

We were lucky in many ways. One of the owners was in the food supply business. He had lobster, steak, you name it. There was no power to save it. I became the official cook with that big family background. I did lunch and dinner for all. Most every condo had a grill, and I used the fuel from all. I knew they would want to share.

The Arab men came but did not bring their wives. I said, "You must bring them. They need food too." They said no, but I made platters for them to take, and they did.

About the third night, one said to me, "How are you doing, Mrs. Schramm? You are doing all the cooking, but you are out cleaning all day for everyone not here and also cleaning the property. Are you okay?"

I just could not sleep. I said, "There is a lot of looting of stores for food. Men are just trying to feed their wives and children. What choice do they have? We are really one of the few buildings with a roof. We are gated, but that means nothing. We cannot close it with no power."

"Mrs. Schramm, please check out your back doors, and every five minutes, you will see either me or my brother patrolling with our rifles over our shoulders. Our stores have not been bothered, either. The community knows we take care of ourselves. You are now our family."

Sure enough, I watched. He was as good as his word.

We were there ten days after the storm. This was a time I saved a life of a choking person. The wife of the manager, Hazel, was eating steak at the other end from where I was, a good twenty feet. I looked at her, and I saw panic in her eyes.

I called to the men down there, "What is wrong with Hazel?" They just looked at me.

There was no time to lose. I ran down and saw her choking. I grabbed her under the ribs and lifted. Nothing happened.

She was a big woman, and at that time, I weighed about 110 pounds. Now there was a ledge up to the apartment. I pulled her the three feet or so over, and I got up above and gave a real jerk up over that ledge, and up came the meat. Usually when you lift, the pressure under the ribs usually forces the object up.

She acted as if nothing happened and told me she was only supposed to eat soft food. I could have then killed her myself.

I said, "I would have made you something soft."

She said, "But it looked so good."

That was my second save. I did two more.

A couple of months later, Bud and I decided to go down to Saint Croix to see what we could do to help out with the damage. We went to LaGuardia Airport, and Bud went up to check us in. We did not have to take anything, as we had everything, and nothing inside our unit had been damaged.

I was standing, waiting for him, when a young tall, elegant, and handsome man walked over to talk to me. He asked me, "Are you going to Saint Croix?"

I said yes. He introduced himself Walt "Clyde" Frazier. What a star, a Hall of Famer for the New York Knicks basketball team. He had carried in a ten-foot curtain rod. His house had been almost completely destroyed. You could buy hardly anything in Saint Croix. What was left in stores had been sold.

We talked about how scared we were and how lucky that no one had died. I knew one little dark secret, though, about deaths from Hugo. I had taken the pilot to the hospital for his ear infection and had seen them put a body bag in the back of a station wagon.

The hospital was a mess—no water or electricity. Blood was everywhere. There was so much destruction, and electricity was not back for many months. It was total madness to see people without homes, having lost everything.

Walt had one of the most breathtaking homes on the island, just over from Buccaneer Golf Resort and Buck Island. Buck Island is the most famous national snorkeling and diving spot in the Caribbean. Snorkeling is an unbelievable thing to do.

We all admired him for the sports but more for the way he would stand with all the kids who would go to the airport to see him. He would stand with these kids and talk with them and never seemed to be in a hurry.

Those kids are now grown men, and I am sure they will never forget his gentility and the time given to them. What an inspiration. He picked that island for tranquility and escape, and the local people respected that.

We were used to seeing him in our neighborhood East Forty-Eighth and Third Avenue in his Rolls-Royce with the plate "Clyde" at a dining spot—Manny Wolf's, now Smith & Wollensky, located at Forty-Ninth and Third Avenue.

Vicki divorced her husband and went to Fairfield, Connecticut, to live with Mary and Scott with her son, Jason. He was pretty much out of control. Vicki would not punish him for anything. He was plain mean to Michael.

Mary and I were sitting talking, and I could see out through the window where the boys were playing in the yard one day. Jason picked up a two-by-four and had it over Michael's head.

I screamed, "Put that board down!"

He threw it down. I went out to get him. Two months before, I had cut a tiny piece of a limb and gave a warning to Jason. I told him how my mother kept one and she only used it once on my legs. I told him how bad it stung. I told him if he hurt Michael one more time, the switch would be on top of the refrigerator, and Mary would use it.

I told Jason, "It really stings badly. You will never forget it."

I took the switch down in front of him and told him to go upstairs and take off his pants and that I would be up. He was crying, begging, and telling me he would never do it again.

I said, "You have promised many times. Now you get the punishment."

I went up the stairs, and he was really crying hard. I knew I had to do it because he could have killed that day. I put red marks across the back of his legs.

I told him, "When your mother comes home, you are to tell what I did and show her, but then you have to tell her why."

She came home shortly and asked where he was. I told her, and she went up. I thought she would come back down and be mad, but she did not say a word.

I got home that night and told Bud what had happened, and he had worried so about Jason and knew he was out of control. I told him that she would probably call and complain about me. She never mentioned it, and Jason never hit Michael again. The switch stayed on top of that refrigerator for a long time.

I put Vicki and Mary in a business. It was a children's resale shop that later also added new clothing. Mary did the buying and pricing, and Vicki ran the shop. She only kept it open from 10:00 a.m. until 5:00 p.m.

Of course, most young mothers held down jobs, so the hours were not good for shopping for their children. We kept it open for two years.

Vicki left, and Mary had three children who were young, so they closed it down. I lost money, but at least the opportunity was there for Vicki to be able to spend more time with her son, Jason, who badly needed to be with her.

CHAPTER 11

The Last Trip with Bud, but the Best

1990 was a good year in so many ways. During a great summer, we went to Hamburg, Germany. We had a great time. Bud said he felt his heritage, and I swear he looked more German than he ever did before. He bought a fisherman's hat and nodded hello like all the natives. We drove down to the seaside, which was about an hour away.

One of the funny things was one morning when he said, "Let's go see the brothels that are so famous."

I laughed and said, "Bud, you are supposed to go there without me."

He said, "You know, I am not going there to participate, but we should see it."

I laughed.

We took a car service there and got out. I must have been one of the rare women to get out there except for the workers.

The guard said, "She cannot go in."

Bud said, "Well, we do not want to be customers; we just want to see it."

We crawled back in the car. At least he could tell his friends he had been there.

I will tell you as all Americans know who have driven the Autobahn that Americans drive very carefully when there—safe to us but an aggravation to them, I am sure.

We were going down to a seashore town, and cars were whizzing by us at what seemed like well over a hundred miles per hour. Bud went fifty miles per hour, trying to stay out of their way. We went to a wonderful place for lunch and started talking to some fellows. They wanted to know where we were from, so we told them.

Bud asked, "How long did it take you to get here from Hamburg?"

They said, "Twenty-five minutes."

I said, "So you were probably the ones that almost blew us off the Autobahn."

They laughed.

Bud bought a couple of pins from Germany and put them on his new hat. He loved wearing it, and he now really fit in with the natives.

I have worn that hat in every Macy's Thanksgiving Day Parade since he died and always will in tribute to him. Each year, I put on a new Macy's pin.

We were in Germany when the Berlin Wall fell. We called American Express about going into Berlin to witness. They told us not to even try, as there would no rooms for miles. We took their advice. I did get to see it several years later when I was on a trip with Peace Links.

It was a glorious trip, and little did I know that it would be our last trip together.

We went back and to our usual going out and having fun.

November always had the excitement of doing the transportation for the Macy's Thanksgiving Day Parade, which was always so much fun, although it was lots of work in a short period of time.

Denise, Bud's mother, had never been to the Macy's Thanksgiving Day Parade, so I insisted that year that she come in and go to the parade, with our usual Thanksgiving dinner after Bud finished up his work. She loved it and was amazed at what went into it. She of course had not seen all the work that went into it from watching it on TV.

I was so happy I requested her presence, as it was the last Thanksgiving we would all have together. All the kids were there. Denise was happy too. She felt bad after seeing how many hours Bud put in that we had always had to drive to North Haven after the parade for dinner at her home.

There would sit Ray and Bob Schramm with their families, having drinks and appetizers. She had always insisted that Bud carve the turkey because he was the oldest. She did it to honor him. I felt sorry, because I knew how tired he was even though I always drove out. Bud never complained, as he also felt it was an honor.

All our workers from Theatrical Teamsters Local 817, Macy's personnel, and anyone involved are like kids. It was no different if it was rain, snow, or a bright, sunny day—the show would go on with all pulling their share.

It was a tired bunch when we finished, but all were happy with another good parade. People throughout the world were being entertained while the turkey cooked. It was especially great to see all those kids along the parade line with wonderment on their faces, and I might add that a lot of adults seemed to become children again.

The next thing memorable was the Theatrical Teamsters Local 817 Christmas party at the Garden City Hotel every year. We saw people we had not since the party the year before. They always did it in style. It was not to be missed.

For that party, Bud had bought a new suit, and I thought he just looked so handsome. Of course, that was not unusual, but it always stuck with me about that party. That was on or about December 16, 1990.

The big rush of getting ready for Christmas was always fun. We had started having it at Mary and Scott's home, as they had three very young children and Vicki with her son. Santa had to come to their houses.

With four grandchildren to buy for, I did have fun shopping, wrapping, and thinking how much fun it would be to see them tearing into the packages. The living room floor was covered. We were planning to drive up to Fairfield, Connecticut, on the twenty-fourth for dinner and put gifts under the tree.

Valerie would also be there. All would be together, and we always had fun watching the kids and had good food, as Mary and Scott are very good cooks, and they made a great party for all.

Our plans were to leave on the twenty-sixth for Saint Croix. We had everything there we needed, but Bud had packed a little bag.

We went out to dinner on the twenty-first to a neighborhood place, Christo's on East Forty-Ninth, now called San Martin. We had a nice dinner with lots of talk about Christmas and then wanting to get down to the sun and play some golf.

On December 22, Bud was not feeling great. I asked the usual question—was there pain anywhere in particular.

He said no. He napped in the afternoon, and we had dinner at home. We did not stay up late.

We both read a lot, so we went to sleep around midnight. The good-night kiss and the "I love you" were never, ever missed.

On Sunday mornings, he always went down to pick up the *Times* and breakfast rolls. I woke up, and he was not in bed, so I assumed he had gone on the normal breakfast run. I showered and dressed, and he was still not home.

I waited awhile, and I was now saying to myself, "Where would he go on a Sunday morning and be so long?"

I went to his bathroom door, and it was closed. I knocked. There was no answer. I opened the door, and my world and his had ended at the young age of sixty-four. He had been reading, sitting in his robe. Glasses lay on the floor, and the book was on his lap. I hurriedly checked for a pulse, and there was none.

I ran and called 911 and then the doorman. He was a young kid, maybe twenty years old, and he was in the apartment in two minutes. He grabbed my hand and took me to the living room. He kept talking in the most soothing voice and never turned loose until the seventeenth precinct arrived. I was in such shock. Nothing was registering with me.

I called Rick Schramm, Bud's cousin to whom he was very close, more like a brother to Bud than his own brother. He got here so quick, but nothing was registering with me.

Mary, Vicki, and Valerie all arrived within an hour. Rick made calls to all the family and friends. The apartment was filled very soon with all. The days were a blur.

He'd had a massive heart attack, and the doctor assured me that he never knew what hit him. The doctor also told me that it wouldn't have mattered if I had been with him; it would have been impossible for me to do anything to save him. It was instant.

I am thankful he did not suffer, and if he had a choice he would have chosen to go quickly. Thank God we had talked about all our interests, and everything was well understood and in our wills. We never thought it would be needed so soon. If I could have had another conversation, it would only to have been to say, "I love you."

Between us, there was never a reason to say we were sorry.

A few weeks before, he had asked me to bring out one of the rings in my sample case that he knew I loved. It is a freshwater pearl; it was very large and museum quality. I could never sell it, as it was expensive. A top designer had made it, and it was the last piece she designed before retiring. They said the pearl was found in a river in Tennessee, and it had taken at least one hundred years to grow. Bud put it on my finger and said, "It should be yours." So it was.

I still wear it daily, and many people ask about it. I get to tell the story often of how it became mine.

Sometimes I tell a story about it that really had me upset. I was driving up the East River Drive, and I noticed the ring was missing. I pulled off at the first chance I had and looked through the car. No luck. I called my office and said, "Please look for it."

No luck there, either.

I had to go on to my appointment but was really anxious to get back to look. It was the last gift he had given me, and it was not something I could go and replace. I tore the apartment apart. No ring.

That night, I got ready to go to bed. I started to undress, and lo and behold, off with the panty hose, and out fell the ring. I could not believe it. I was one happy person. I was always sure if it got a little loose to make sure the guard was right.

I will always wonder if Bud had a premonition of what was going to happen. It was not unusual, but we were standing in our kitchen about two weeks before, and he had taken me in his arms, kissed me, and said, "I want you to know I have never loved another woman in my life. You have my heart totally." I treasure that moment.

Campbell Funeral Home had taken care of Bud's father's funeral arrangements, so that of course was the easiest of the decisions I had to make. Campbell told me there could be no funeral until after Christmas.

Well, I guess that was good, because my family had to travel from Arkansas and other parts of the country. I was numb, so I never questioned anything I was told, as I was past making decisions except the ones I had to face.

On Christmas Eve, Mary and Scott insisted they take me to Fairfield for the kids. They packed up everything, and we went. This was very good thinking on their part. I was comatose. Scott made me a drink when we arrived at their house. Of course, I did not even taste it. He refilled before it was empty.

I had not slept. I said I was going to lie down a few minutes. I guess I passed out from pure exhaustion. I do not remember much.

I picked out the new suit that he had looked so good in at the Christmas party, and he had worn it to the dinner we attended on the twenty-first.

Two things happened that really bothered me at the funeral and wake. As I walked in, I saw his ex and two daughters down at the casket. It was open. We both had put in papers that our caskets were to be closed. Valerie and I talked about it, so she knew. I was mortified. I had let his wishes be broken but had told the funeral home to keep it closed. I went to them, and they apologized and said the daughters had begged them to open it for a minute. I made no scene and just asked them to close it. They did.

I walked into the funeral parlor for the wake. Bud's ex-wife was there holding court. He paid her every week for twenty-seven years and hated every time he had to write the check, and then he had to take papers down to the IRS to prove it, because he gave so much of his income, they did not understand how he could do it. They made him take all records for many years.

I let that pass, and our close friends were ticked. It was not like she was there for young children for their support twenty-seven years after the divorce.

The next was after the services, and we were going on that long trip to Sag Harbor for interment.

There was Bud's ex-wife again asking our friends, who had also once been hers, to get a ride with them to the interment. At that point, one of Bud's longtime friends told her to get lost.

"Nadine is the widow," he said.

Bud had told me of when his father had died, and he had to pick out clothing for his father. He took shoes, and the man at the funeral home had said, "We will not need these you can take them home." Bud said that was the heaviest bag he had ever carried in his life. I sent shoes, and I would have insisted they be used. They did not ask.

Picking out the casket was so hard. Music was easy—music from Frank Sinatra, the Metropolitan Opera, and also the New York Philharmonic. "I Did It My Way" by Frank was one of Bud's favorites, and he did live it his way. I always say he lived three lives in one.

Denise, Bud's mother, had lost her husband much too young and then Bud when he was so young. She told me losing a son was much worse. No mother should have to bury her child. Denise never remarried and always said no one could compare to Louie. I thought when I met her it was such a shame, as she was fun, attractive, and knew how to live. She loved to dance, and I always said she glided, not walked, across the floor, even in her own home.

Today, I fully understand what she meant. I have come to have the same feeling. I had such a bad experience with Tom and then went on to have a most wonderful marriage with Bud; I have never thought of marrying again. I now know she probably wished she could meet someone who could change her mind, but that is difficult when you have been so happy.

When I went to Campbell Funeral Home, they showed

me a huge yellowed folder of Bud's father's funeral. They told me it was the largest they had ever had, and it still held as the largest in 1990. Lines went a whole block around the home for hours, and they had to allow only a couple of minutes at the casket. Agents came from all over the country.

Twenty years after Bud's father's death, there was always a moment of silence for him at Allied conventions. I could not believe it when sitting there.

One day, I said to Bud, "I know your father was a great man, but I am tired of no one ever saying it to you. Bud, you have done a good job following him. I want you to know I think you have been equally as good. You have helped to support three widows and one's four children. He never had to do that."

Tears came to his eyes, and he said, "You are the only one that has said anything to that effect. Thank you so much."

I am happy I told him, and it was the truth.

Oh, if we could have just stretched it out, but it was not to be.

I remember very little, as I was in shock, and although I did all I had to do. It was if someone else was just pushing me though the horror.

We had only a couple of years before we lost a good

friend, and we went to his wake and funeral at Yardley, Sag Harbor. I said to Bud, "When the wake is over, let's go in and set up an appointment to buy a plot. Whoever thought we would be going to this funeral of our friend?"

"We can do it another time," he said.

I said, "No. It will be easy. We are here."

Reluctantly, he went in with me. We went in, and he immediately went outside for a cigarette. I said, "I can't believe he went out."

Mr. Yardley laughed and said, "The men all do that."

We made an appointment for the next morning to pick out a plot, and Mr. Yardley asked if we had any preference of where. I did not care. Bud said, "The highest ground available."

One of the first times I had gone to Sag Harbor with Bud, he had taken me on a tour. One of the places he took me was to the cemetery. It has lots of old graves of sailors from whaling days. One was called the broken mast. It is a huge broken mast dedicated to all who went down at sea, never to return, and it had no names on it; it was just dedicated to unknown sailors.

When we went the next morning to pick out the plot, where did Mr. Yardley take us? Just down from the mast, across the small road from where Balanchine, the great choreographer, is buried. That grave was beautifully maintained with the whole grave always planted with wonderful flowers, watered and cared for with what had to be great love.

I was so happy. I had insisted on looking at plots and buying; otherwise, we would have had to just take them sight unseen.

Cemeteries have always been interesting to me. I love to walk through and look at names, birth years, and death years. Many times, you see children who died young, and you feel the pain of the parents and siblings as I saw in my family—that link missing in a family chain that can never be replaced. It has a great impact on all members. In our case, it was Martha losing her twin.

I will say here I learned a very valuable lesson with all this having to do things under such stress. In about two years, I made an appointment with Campbell's. I told them I wanted to make arrangements for my funeral, whenever that may be.

When we met, I said I wanted the same kind of casket as Bud or similar if his was no longer available. Everything else was to be the same. I set up preplan payment. All was taken care of. I want no one to have to do that for me. Everyone should do it that way.

Death is really as sure as taxes. Why not make preparation for the funeral, as it is really not painful? I sat and chatted with the young lady at Campbell Funeral Home for a long time. I left there feeling I had done something good. No one should have to make that awful trip to a funeral home.

I could not laugh about this for a long time. When Bud died, the first thing I got was a list of things I must do from the lawyer—papers from safe-deposit boxes or anything I might need. We had two at two different banks. One had coins, and another had cash we kept on hand for business in case of emergency repairs and so on. There were two envelopes with $5,000 each.

Rick and I first went for the coins, and they were heavy but only two blocks away.

As we were walking down for the cash, I said to Rick, "I hope it's gone and he had a ball with it."

Well, I signed in, and he went in with me. I opened the box, and there were the two envelopes, both torn open and empty. I burst out laughing.

I said, "I do hope he had fun." It might have been Atlantic City, or maybe he had used some of it for our trip to Germany. Whatever. I had no regrets it was not there.

The insurance policy was very hard for me. I was called by Mr. Charles Drimal of New York Life to his office to sign papers to collect on policies.

I said, "Let's wait for a few months," and I was informed it needed to be done within a short time. I had the worst feeling that I was taking money for his life. To me, at the time, it just was not good money. I also felt the same about the social security check. Now, of course, I know that is not how one should think. All was paid for.

The ex-wife had no problem. She collected on a policy he had to keep with her as the beneficiary from the divorce proceedings. Even the insurance man said, "Boy, she wanted that money fast."

On January 1, she had gone to social security office to collect. She had been his wife for ten years; therefore, she felt was eligible to collect. She was there a month before I was. At first, the lady taking care of me got mixed up said I had already applied. I told her that, no, it was just the ex who had. I'm glad I have never been that needy or greedy. Anyway, that is just part of life, and we all handle things differently. None of that had any effect on my life.

There was another thing, but this took me much longer to laugh about. We, as I said earlier, had been to a dinner at a local place on December 21, which I mentioned before, when they told me to cancel all credit cards. I looked for Bud's American Express and could not find it. I called American Express, and I was telling them I needed to cancel his card but could not find it. The woman was very nice and said, "Do you by any chance know when he might have used it last?"

It dawned on me that it must have been at that restaurant, Christo's. I told her and got off the phone. I knew I had sent Bud to heaven with an American Express card in his pocket in that brown suit. They always say do not leave home without it. Well, everything must have been free, because he did not use it. I could not joke about it for a number of years. He would have loved it, and he would have laughed too.

In our Turtle Bay neighborhood, we had a wonderful association called Turtle Bay Association, which helped keep everyone up to date with issues of the day. It was well organized with its news publication and very dedicated. It monitored what was happening with buildings and had a tree fund, which helped to have trees planted on all the streets in the district.

I love animals but sometimes felt sorry for large dogs that needed open spaces to run. Many times, they do not live as long as they should without that exercise. We also had a problem with some dog owners thinking their dogs should be able to urinate on these trees. That kills them slowly but surely.

Katherine Hepburn, who spent much of her life in the neighborhood and owned an apartment on Forty-Ninth between Second and Third, loved gardens and was very instrumental with the Turtle Bay Association in the cleanup of the Dag Hammarskjold Plaza between First and Second Avenue by the United Nations.

The plaza was named after Dag Hammarskjold, a president of the United Nations who died an untimely death while working there. The park was a disgrace and just up from the UN. City buses parked with engines running all the time, and they parked where it was dirt, making deep ruts. The grass was rarely cut. It was an unsightly mess.

It is now one of the most beautiful, pristine parks in the city, with an area called Katherine Hepburn Gardens, a separate walkway featuring her sayings and beautiful plants and flowers. Volunteers and city workers did much to keep it clean. The park is filled with beautiful benches for all to sit and read or visit. It also is used for many concerts, community affairs, and more.

When Bud passed away, I put up a beautiful memorial in his name in the park that depicts the movie *On Golden Pond*, with the etching of Katherine and all the stars. We saw her many times in our neighborhood, sometimes with Spencer Tracy, as she lived just a block away from our building. You could never forget that strong face.

Bud had always loved her movies, and I knew he would be very happy to have his name on a plaque to commemorate her. I walk through often. I had hoped others from the neighborhood would follow with plaques. Maybe some will after reading about my experience and know it is an available option.

Now my life was in total state of change. I had a hard time. I did not sleep. I walked the floor, waiting for sunup. There was no time to slack from work, which was a good thing. I had no time to feel sorry for myself. There was just a feeling of such a void in my world, losing someone who was such a strong influence on my every day and night and who had given me so much to be thankful for.

I did not need to fear anyone, as I always felt so secure in my life with him. It was not that I was that needy, but it was comforting just to know I never had to worry about a mean word or action. I had always been able to adjust and do things, but this was a total reorganization.

Sometimes I felt his presence. This may sound strange to some, but it did not seem to be unusual to me. Once, early in the morning hours, I had a dream that I will never forget; it was so real. I saw Bud sitting on a couch in our office.

He said to me, "Please take care of Mom."

I said, "Of course I will," and I started toward him.

There was a loud swishing sound, and he was gone.

I woke up but tried hard to go back to sleep, thinking he would again reappear. He did not, but it was still very vivid in my memory.

CHAPTER 12

Success, with Help from Many Great People

When Bud had started the business, I did all his billing and helped in all ways I could in the evenings. Bud's daughter Valerie was working for us when Bud died. I could not depend on her for any help. She had been working with Bud for about four years, so she really could have helped me during this very stressful time.

Our wills read exactly the same: whoever survived was 100 percent owner. I now had a will that was not of any good, since Bud was my named beneficiary. One of Bud's cousins by marriage, a lawyer, was helping me to make a new will. I was having a hard time. I told him what was going on with Valerie. Her sister was with her on it, but not in the same way. She was just a follower.

He told me, "Nadine, with what is going on with the hurt and anger, just write them out, and if they change, you can rewrite it any time to include them."

I was losing lots of sleep, and the stress was showing on me.

I was also losing my hair in large amounts.

I closed down my business, as mine had no employees. Many people worked for Budd Enterprises. At the funeral, I had a few who asked me what would happen to Budd Enterprises. I had not even thought of that.

I remember saying, "You will have a job. Those trucks have Bud's name on them, and they will continue to be on the streets."

I had no idea of when the contracts would end. I went into the files, and they had a while to run.

June was the date for the concerts in the parks. I had gone to all since I began dating Bud, and I loved them. I knew all the people involved with the concerts, but they knew me just as Bud's wife. I was not even sure they knew I had a business. One thing I did know was that a new outdoor stage had been built. It weighed ninety thousand pounds. It had been sent to upstate New York for repairs. They had done a test run only and had found things to be repaired. During one of our dinners, Bud had told me he was worried about bringing the stage back down the mountains, afraid the brakes might burn out, which would be a disaster. To me, the driver's life was the most important, but then there would be millions lost in equipment if damaged or totaled.

My first question when there is an accident is "Are there any injuries?" Any equipment can be replaced, but a life cannot.

I had just taken over when Bud passed away, and this was a very unusual job because of the weight of the stage coming down through the mountains. That's what I was thinking in April when I was doing the planning for these concerts and bringing the stage down. I wasn't worried about the concerts at all.

Well, just before we were to pick it up, I talked to Mike Hyde, the Theatrical Teamsters Local 817 captain on the job, and I said, "Listen, Mike, if the brakes fail, turn the wheels to the right and bail out."

He laughed and said, "We think the same."

Mike helped me so much that first year and many following. He came down those mountains gingerly with no problems. He was seasoned. He had learned from his father, Harold, who had been captain on those concerts for several years before his retirement.

Valerie had evidently snooped within our personal papers, because she knew before the will was read what it stipulated, and she was mad, because she knew she was not a beneficiary.

There was one thing Bud and I understood about each

other, and it was our code of ethics. We trusted each other with any decisions we made.

Valerie would come to the office maybe by 10:00 a.m. and leave for lunch at noon and then an afternoon therapy appointment at 3:00 p.m. She hardly said good morning or good night to me. This was so different from our relationship with her before Bud's death. Never before was an unkind word spoken between us.

Valerie went to our lawyer, Henry Clay, and tried to contest the will, but she was told she had no chance. Both wills were written at exactly the same time by Henry.

So, finally, I said to her, "Look, we are all hurting badly. You lost a father, and I lost a husband, but we have to continue on."

She looked at me and said, "Yes, they sure have changed, and I am not happy."

I said, "What is the problem?"

She told me she thought she should have gotten 50 percent of her father's assets. I was stunned even though I already knew.

I said, "Valerie, we have wills. They are the same. This is how it works."

Wills are made for people to say how their wishes are to be done. Valerie stated that she had worked for the company about four years and therefore deserved it.

I said, "You were paid well."

Everyone I was dealing with was concerned about me. They asked me about anything that was bothering me and if they could help. They also had noticed Valerie never being at the office. I told them what was going on. They were furious.

They said, "You have been a caring mother to them. This does not play."

This attitude continued, and I was running the business as well as dealing with lawyers, insurance, accountants, and most of all, the loss of a man I loved with all my heart.

I finally realized I had to make changes. I told Valerie I wanted her to take two weeks off with pay. I needed time alone.

She said, "I do not want to take my vacation now."

I said, "This is just paid time off. It has nothing to do with your vacation."

She said, "I will think about it."

I looked at her and said, "Do you see the chair I am sitting in? This is the chair of the owner of this company. You have forced my hand. I do not care how you spend the two weeks, but it is not to be here. I need time alone."

She huffed out. I did all the work and did not feel that extra pressure. I also found that I could do all the work. It was much easier than dealing with her attitude.

The time went by, and on the Friday before she was to be back on Monday, she called to inform me she was at a ski resort out west and was going to stay until Wednesday because the ski area was so great.

This sent me over the edge, and I had no problem saying, "I do not want to do this over the phone, but since you are having such a good time, I will tell you my plans. I have found I can run the business and have been since your father passed away, without any help from you. So why not just stay there and enjoy the beautiful snow."

She remarked, "You are firing me?"

"No. I just do not need you."

I got a letter telling me all the things she wanted from our apartment—the most important pieces in our home. One thing in particular was a bronze of Chief Crazy Horse. It had been in their home in the bar area. Bud had left with his clothes and very little else. His ex-wife hated the Indian and asked him to take it out after a while. He had brought it to his little apartment, and I loved it. We happened to see the same bronze in a museum in Denver, Colorado. They insisted we could not have one of the same.

Bud said, "I will send you a picture," and then they contacted us to say it was authentic, which we already knew. I found it interesting that Valerie wanted it. I had researched it. It was a valuable bronze. That did not matter to us so much, but it was an important piece in our home. I made it so by personally making a stand for it so it had a special place. We both loved it, not for the value but for its beauty.

Another item she wanted was a ring he always wore. Since I had been in the jewelry business, I had decided I would take the ring and have it duplicated. It is done with the old-world wax process. I knew both the girls had seen it on his hand for all their lives and I had from the day I met him. With that process, you could not tell the original. I planned to put them in a bag and let each would take one.

Valerie said, "I want the original." Should she have it over her sister? I felt not. I still have the ring. When you try your best and someone is still not satisfied, there is nothing else you can do.

What a change in a person. I wrote back and said, "I am still living. When I die, there will be a will." I had no intention of taking pieces out of our apartment.

I could not believe this was really happening. I had been married for twenty-three years, and we had dated for three years prior to that. I was not someone who had married for money. I had more than he did when we married, and we never discussed money. It really did not make any difference to either of us.

It took me a long time to get over that. Now I look

at things in another way. The ones I did the most for are those who thought money and goods would always come to them without questions. I now give to ones who do not expect, and many do not even know I exist. I never give with thoughts of getting something back.

I said to myself that when I married Bud, I gained two daughters. When he died, I lost them at the same time.

My way of coping with something at the time was very painful. One would not think there would be that divide, but there is no doubt that it was simply over money. Lawyers and others told me it happened very often. How sad. They would have done much better to wait, as the picture has much improved over the years.

Bud would have been shocked at their actions. I haven't heard from either of them since. I would not change anything that I did for them. It was a great experience for me. I would have liked the relationship to continue, but so be it. I have learned there are things you have no control over.

Bud had more friends than anyone I had ever known. It was always fun being around him, and he treasured his friends. He called them, keeping in touch always, worrying about their health and never about his own. They were all there for me. Many tears have been shed, but also a lot of laughter had been shared while remembering the good times.

I went to visit three couples in Florida—Jack and Hilda Kirkeby, Irene and Paul Kenwood, and Dottie and Bill Benisch. They made dinner. We were having a good time reminiscing about all our good times together. Bill could imitate Bud to perfection with the way he held his cigarette and held his drink, and he could even imitate Bud's voice. He started to do it, and Jack stopped him, thinking it would upset me.

I said, "No, it actually makes me happy. I never want us to stop laughing and talking the way we always have." Bud had always laughed so hard when Bill had done it.

I rarely cried. Bud saw me cry only a few times, and he got so upset and would beg me not to because he could not stand to see me hurt. When he died, I was so sure he still would know if I did cry. The tears never came. He wasn't there to tell me all would be okay.

Bud had given me so much to be happy about—a life I could never have wished for, as I did not know it existed. If I ever said this to friends, they would say, "You were the perfect partner. You gave him what no one else could. You had the same zest for life and a love so complete that no one else could ever do."

Ralph, my dear brother, got me involved in politics a couple of years after Bud passed away. My whole life had become the business.

My family knew I needed to let loose a little bit, and I did take time for Mary, Scott, and the grandchildren very soon. We all went to our condo for a week's vacation in Saint Croix. It was good just to be with them. The kids loved the beach and pool.

One night when we were standing in the yard looking up at a beautiful star-studded sky, Kelly, my youngest grandchild, wrapped her little arms around herself and said, "Please, Grandpa, come down and hug me." I ran into the condo. I did not want her to see me upset. She would have thought at that age she had done something to hurt me. And if I started to cry, it would not end for me that fast. I sure did not want her to think what she had said was upsetting. It was so touching to see a child express herself with such love and the feeling of loss.

Anyone who knows me well knows I am very strong. I guess all the things I had lived through made me almost numb in many ways. Yet I am such an easy touch for sympathy or helping anyone else with troubles.

Mary had told me when Bud passed she took all three children out in their yard and told them to look up in the sky and pick out a star that was Grandpa looking down. He would always be there for them. I believe he is. It stuck with Kelly, as young as she was.

Michael, my first grandchild, was eight when Bud

passed. They, of course, were with me before the funeral in my apartment. On the calendar, Michael had written on December 23, "Oh no. Grandpa died today."

Michael came by train to see me very often, always with flowers in his hand. He had always spent his allowance on me. I still get more flowers from him than I have from anyone else.

One night, we went to DeGrezia, a restaurant that I went to regularly. When they took us to a table and the waiter started to pull out my chair, Michael said to the waiter, "I will do that." He was much shorter than the back of this heavy chair. He pulled it out with all his strength. A few nights later, I was there, and they said to me, "What a grandson you have. Grown men do not even make the effort."

For men out there, this should be a point very well taken. It is appreciated by many of us no matter how successful and efficient we are in our lives.

Mary and Scott taught all three of their children very good manners when they were young. It still shows today. By the age of two, their manners were better than many adults'.

Amanda, the one who called Bud every day at 5:00 p.m., enjoyed a wonderful relationship with him. It got so that Bud would say, "If it's Amanda, let me have a scotch first." He loved the calls but knew it would be long about her day. It would be twenty minutes of talk. He called her "twerp."

Later, she got in a fight with a schoolmate who called her "twerp." She must have told someone, and word got around.

She was very adamant and said, "No one can call me 'twerp' except for Grandpa."

Amanda held court wherever she went. She was beautiful and sassy at five years old. I might add she still is both.

Mary and Scott loved to cook, so their kitchen was huge, with a counter and a see-though space to a sitting area and playroom so that they could watch the three kids. One day, Michael had a friend over to play. The friend was messing with Amanda, who was five, and she told him twice to stop and if he did not, she would use her karate on him.

Mary heard all this but was busy in the kitchen. The next thing she heard was a tremendous cracking sound. It was the breaking of the boy's nose. Amanda had followed through on her threat. Blood was spurting all over. Mary grabbed a towel, holding it to catch the blood, and she called me. She was really upset, thinking the boy's parents would sue. She called the mother and told her and said, "We will take him to the hospital."

Mary had told her of Amanda's remarks and action. The mother calmly said, "He deserved it." The mother came to pick up her son. That kid went to the same school, and when Amanda started, he told all his friends not to bother her because she would hurt them.

Amanda got it in her head she wanted to take karate at four.

Mary put her in the school. The teacher said he had never had a kid that age who was like her. She got all the belts, and I had seen her practice. She could bring her foot up over her head. It was some sight to watch her.

Mary took her to the instructor for him to explain to her that she should not use it except when she was in danger of someone doing something to hurt her. Amanda explained very expertly that he was doing something wrong. The instructor said he had a hard time keeping a straight face because she was so adamant that she was right in doing what she had done. Word traveled fast not to mess with Amanda.

Mary got pulled over one day for something, and the officer was getting ready to write the ticket. Mary has the three kids buckled in the backseat. The officer looked back there and said, "You're Amanda's mother?" He did not write the ticket. He remembered her from seeing them in the diner they went to.

Mary taught her children the car would not move unless the seat belts were on. They learned very early the necessity of buckling themselves up. It is now law, but it was not back then.

When they came to visit, which was often, I always thought it was a treat for them to get to go to one my favorite restaurants for dinner. I had several, most of which I still go to today.

One night, they were all in the city to visit me. I said, "I am going to make us dinner tonight."

They all three started to laugh, and one spoke up and said, "Grandma, you can cook?"

It dawned on me I was not being the typical grandmother. I cooked, and they loved it. I am a good cook and love dinner parties in my home. At that time and even today, after twenty-three years, I still will not eat at our dining room table alone. It may look to people who only knew me after Bud died that I was lazy about cooking, but it is simply that I have always had lots of people at my table, or at least Bud. No matter what I cooked, when I was alone, the food tasted like cardboard. Those dinners we had cooked together with candlelight and wine, most nights dancing in our living room to Sinatra and others, had spoiled me.

We had seven vehicles when Bud passed away, and most

of them were used at CBS. But remember, he had been in the family business with many more. He was happy slowing down and taking some time off to enjoy life more with less pressure.

My first contract came up with CBS very shortly after Bud died. Now this was going to be a test for me. I went in and made little change to the contract. The usual raise in the price of labor, which was set by the union, was included. I was very happy that they signed. Again, that supposed woman issue seemed not to matter. I had continued to give the service they were used to. I had learned well from Bud. We were much alike in the fact of believing your name would be ruined if you did not live up to promises made.

I was comfortable in my role when I took it over, but it was so different from anything I had ever done. There was constant monitoring of work performed, payroll, and billing that had to be kept up to date. Bills were paid as they came in; that way, I got service from my suppliers first. Payroll was paid weekly. If a man happened to work on Sunday, his pay is made with our regular pay on Tuesday the following week. I never forgot how I lived from week to week.

I do not like to owe money to anyone and have kept the rule my parents lived by. If you do not have the money to pay for something, do not buy it. That included equipment. Some say you need to have borrowing records to be able to borrow. I say you need to have a record of not having to. I bet a lot of people would be a lot better off without a lot of goodies they bought on credit right now.

The personal contact with all customers so they were worry-free about our performance was the most important thing in my business. It is many times overlooked by many business owners, but not in my office. I am personally available 24-7. An assistant is also available 24-7 to handle any problem in the most efficient way possible. Getting a contract may be easy for a good salesperson with a gift of gab, but performance is what holds customers for many years, and that is what we did every day to ensure that confidence.

I was amazed at the help I got from people when I took charge of operations of Budd Enterprises. Although I was a capable businesswoman, the trucking business was different. We talked all the time about our businesses, and I listened intently to him, but I did not know what he really did on a day-to-day basis.

When he started, I had done his paperwork in the evenings after taking care of my own. Now I was wearing out file folders trying to learn everything.

I got a call from what other people would call my competitor, Eugene Walton Sr., owner of Walton Hauling.

He said, "I am a friend of your husband."

I said, "I know who you are."

He said, "If you have anything come up that you do not know the answer to, please call me. I will help in any way I can."

I did call him several times, and he readily walked me through the issue. What a good friend he turned out to be. He also served on the board of Theatrical Teamsters Local 817 with me. He was a fine man. I was very sorry when he passed away. I had lost a good colleague. His son, Gene, was equally as good.

CHAPTER 13

Politics, Business, and Fun

Ralph called me and asked me to come to Little Rock for a party he was having as the president of the Senior Democratic Party. He had invited Senator Gore, Al's father, to be his guest speaker, and he had said yes. So I said I would be there. Ralph said he would make my reservations for the hotel and flight. I wondered why but just thought he knew I was busy and was taking pressure off me.

I got on the flight, which landed in Nashville, Tennessee, to pick up passengers. When we got close to Little Rock, a hostess said, "Mrs. Schramm, we will be landing in a few minutes. I will be back to escort you from the plane."

My heart came up in my throat. I thought something bad must have happened in the family. Sure enough, she came and took me to the front of the plane. When I got off, I was met by another airline employee who told me not to worry about my baggage and to walk with him. Once out of the airport, I saw what was happening.

Senator Gore and his wife were getting into a black SUV with three behind it, all filled with agents. I realized Ralph had arranged it all. The Gores and I introduced ourselves, and they were expecting me. This was my first ride in a motorcade other than funerals. The Gores were so nice and insisted we call each other by first names.

We arrived at the hotel, and I was told, "Your bags will be taken to your room. You are already checked in."

We took a special elevator with agents up to the top floor of the Excelsior Hotel for Ralph, his wife, Nita, Inez, me, and the Gores, who were across from us. They asked us to go down for lunch, and we did. This was the beginning of a fun two days. The first evening was dinner with the Gores, Ralph, Nita, Inez, and me. The Gores were a lovely couple, without big egos.

Inez and I had just gotten undressed for bed when the phone rang. It was the senator.

He said, "Come on over. It is much too early for bed."

"But, Senator, we are already dressed for bed."

"Well, throw on robes and walk across the hall."

There was one little problem. As we opened our door, there were six agents all sitting with their backs up against the wall in the hall, some already sound asleep. Up they jumped, embarrassed. We laughed and said, "Go back to sleep." We knew we were safe, as a key had to be used by them to take us up or down the elevator. When were we ever going to have that kind of protection again?

We had a nice time as Southerners getting acquainted. Mrs. Gore told how us she was from Texarkana, Arkansas, and was a lawyer out of school when she met the senator. She married and moved to Tennessee. Then they went to Washington, DC, when he became a senator. They went home to Tennessee when he left Washington and politics. Their son, Al Gore Jr., had grown up in Washington, DC. Now he was vice president, and they were proud parents.

The next morning, we got an early call saying, "Come on over. The senator is making breakfast." Of course, we went, and sure enough, he was making eggs, bacon—the whole works—in the kitchen of their suite.

That morning, I was lucky to get pictures of the Gores with President Bill Clinton's mother and stepfather together.

Ralph again had given a great party.

I was invited to the Gores' farm in a little town in Tennessee. It was a shame I did not go, and therefore, I missed another fun time with lovely people. But I do treasure those two days.

A year after Bud died, Ralph called me up and said, "Nadine, I want to talk to you," and he came to New York.

I said, "Yes, Ralph, what is it?"

He was worried about me and thought I was pouring too much of myself into business and was taking no time for any pleasure. He said he thought I should start thinking about dating and that I was still young and attractive. He said I should be out there.

I said, "Ralph, I have not even thought about that, and I do not know if I ever will. But I am certainly not ready yet."

He said, "I do not mean you should go out with some old fart who just wants to read the paper and watch television."

I broke out laughing. I said, "Well, that will never happen, even if I ever date. I am not attracted to that type of person."

I was surprised, because our family never told each other what to do, but my brother was just worried about me, and it was very sweet that he was.

I did get very involved with Ralph in the political world. He was involved when Governor Bill Clinton started his run for the presidency. Now that excited me to think that Arkansas might have one of our own in the White House as president of the United States. I went to both election nights in Arkansas and then to both conventions and both inaugurals.

I went to the first inaugural with Ralph; the next was more exciting because of the kids. I took eight to the second inaugural: my daughter, Mary; her husband, Scott; their children Michael, Amanda, and Kelly; John Miller, owner of Archimboldo's, one of the most beautiful Italian restaurants in New York; and friends from Boston.

The first election night in Arkansas was the most exhilarating. Ralph and my sister-in-law Nita are wonderful hosts.

We went to a party in Dale Bumpers's suite for Bill Clinton in the Excelsior Hotel. Then we had an invitation to the statehouse, next door to our hotel, for the announcement he had won. Well, we went down, but Little Rock is a small town, and the crowds were big. It was also very windy. They had horses for crowd control, and it was almost impossible to move.

I said to our group, "Let's go back upstairs. We can look right down, and we will see more from there."

Everyone agreed, and up we went. When that was over, there was a party upstairs in the ballroom. We were invited to that also. We went up, and the crowd, needless to say, was thrilled, laughing, singing, and having a ball.

We saw on monitors that Bill Clinton had come into

the lobby. President Bill Clinton was noted for shaking every hand stuck out to him and having a conversation to go with it. This went on and on.

Well, after some time, we were anxious to share this moment in history. Someone went to the microphone and said, "We all know how to get his attention. Let's do the hog call." (That is the Razorbacks' football call.)

He could hear from the monitors downstairs. We started the call. He looked up at us and bounded up the stairs. We went crazy shouting when he walked in the room.

A fun thing I arranged was a trip to Washington, DC, for a party honoring Senator Dale Bumpers. I knew that President Bill Clinton and First Lady Hillary were going to be at the reception and dinner.

I rented a bus from a company that did jobs for the movie industry to take us to DC. It held twenty-six people and had a bar and bathrooms. I called friends who I knew would appreciate the trip. I also invited three players from the WNBA's New York Liberty team. I thought they would add to the trip, and they did. We all met at my building, and away we went.

I had made all the arrangements, and the person handling the account said they knew how to get to DC and the hotel. I went to DC fairly often but always by train, so I had no idea of exits or route to hotel.

It started to rain heavily, and I was concerned, as the bus was not as heavy duty as I would have liked. There was much swaying around, and I felt very much responsible for everyone.

We had drinks, laughed, and had a great time. It was black tie, and we had all carried our dresses to get dressed on the bus. We took turns in the bathrooms. You can guess the scene with that many women dressing for black tie. We did it and had lots of fun. The guys just used the bus, and we turned our heads.

When we got down close to DC, the driver wanted to know what exit he should take. I said, "You mean you do not have directions?"

He said no.

Now we had to try to find out which one to take, and it was raining harder than ever. We were also now running late. I knew the system, and if we did not get there before the president, we would not get in, or at best, we would face very awkward security questions.

We started calling people to see if we could find out the exit. We finally pulled up, and it was just a few minutes until the event started. With the help of the Bumperses, we got in.

Well, everyone got to meet the president and others. What a night. That was early in his presidency, and there was a very small crowd of about 150. Everyone got their picture taken with him.

We all had to be back to work the next morning, so it was back on the bus to make that long trip home, but everyone was happy.

Betty Bumpers called and invited me to go to Sun Valley. We had a group of five women, and none of us were skiers. We had a great time, and I had never been there. One night, we went on a tour of homes, and there are many beautiful ones.

Then we went to dinner with plans to go to a diner that was very popular for its desserts. We were in an SUV, and of course, I was always speeding, so I was out and up to the steps, and they were still back by the car.

As I started up the steps, two guys stepped out the door and blocked my way. They had not shaved in three days and had on torn blue jeans. One was asking me all kinds of questions about my evening and if I was having fun and so on. I was not really interested in talking to them and kind of tried to push past them with no luck. I was pleasant but not saying much.

Finally, they moved on. The girls came up, and they were laughing and asking me if I knew who was talking to me. I said, "Two ski bums, no doubt."

It was Bruce Willis, who was doing the talking, and a

friend. He had just broken up with Demi Moore. He was either celebrating or hurting.

One of the most successful events running Budd Enterprises I had to handle early on was a concert for Luciano Pavarotti, the Italian opera singer who had become one of the most successful tenors of all time.

In June 1993, I was contacted by Carolyn Ferrell of the Metropolitan Opera regarding the concert, which was to be held in Central Park. Of course, this was very exciting, but I knew it would be huge and require a lot of planning. It would be handled by a management group out of Australia.

A gentleman was sent a month in advance to work out details. The Met was not involved, but Carolyn was very well versed on how the planning should be handled because of her experience running the concerts in the park. She was a very much needed help to me.

She and I had many meetings with this Australian to try to get some kind of schedule. Nothing was forthcoming. He would just say he did not have the plans yet. This was not something you put together in a couple of days. The Parks Department as well as other officials of the city had to be in on the planning. Without any of their plans, it was impossible to work out a schedule, and we had no other contacts to work with us.

Now I had to contact the Teamster union, and they named the captain that would handle the job, Peter Tavis.

Three days before the date, two men arrived who were the head bosses of the Australian firm. They met with us, and we informed them that we had been given no information from their lead man. They were dumbfounded. They said, "We will pull it together," and they did, but we really had to scramble.

As planned, we used the big stage that was owned by the Met and the New York Philharmonic. That was the one thing we knew from the beginning. You had to see how hard the men worked to put all together like clockwork.

Now I had a little problem with how I was going to collect for this large job. I knew after the concert they would all be on their way back to Australia. My expenses would be very high, so I told the two gentlemen I needed to get paid as we progressed.

They agreed, and I started giving them handwritten bills that Pete Tavis and I put together. Then they just stood and wrote out checks.

On the day of the concert, the lighting guys were up on poles putting up the lights. Their union officials came over to me and said, "Nadine, how are you going to be paid?" I told them I was being paid almost by the minute, as when they left town, I did not want to have to chase them for payment.

"How do you do that?" they asked.

"See your guys up on those poles? Bring them down, and they will want to talk to you. Tell them you need some payment. Just don't tell them I told you to ask."

Sure enough, the bosses came to me instead of them and asked me what was going on.

I said, "I don't know, but over there are their union officials."

Needless to say, they again brought out their checkbooks. Up the poles the men went and finished the job.

It was very interesting to watch the rehearsal with Pavarotti in a Hawaiian shirt with a red bandana around his neck. He was very much overweight and had been told by his doctor to lose a lot of weight. I asked his manager if he had lost it. His reply was "Nadine, he could lose ten pounds off one arm and you would not notice."

Well, the night of the concert was an unbelievable sight. Five hundred thousand people poured into the Great Lawn in Central Park. Speakers had been put out so all could hear. The concert was televised, so millions more saw and heard that great voice.

Now Peter and I stood behind the stage and counted

hours and men. When the show ended, I knew there would be little to collect. Sure enough, when we added the last little bit, we were owed seventeen dollars.

I was asked to come to their hotel the next morning to get final payment. They laughed and said they had enjoyed working with me. They said they had never worked with anyone so efficient with billing. I thanked them for being just as good in paying.

One thing was so funny, but I almost felt sorry for him. The guy who had done nothing in the planning was made to fold up about one hundred chairs that were for special guests by himself. They told me he had to earn his pay for the month of doing nothing.

We were lucky with Pavarotti. He was known for cancelations sometimes very shortly before he was to perform. He died much too young of pancreatic cancer. The date was September 6, 2007. He gave much to the music world and will always be remembered by me and as one of the top entertainers I have ever seen and listened to.

In 1994 I started going down to Atlantic City to get away from business. When you play slots, you are mindless. I always stayed at Bally's Park Place. I also loved to play blackjack; it is slow, though, but I had always been able to play for hours. I would lose no money but not make any, either. Slots were a lot faster. They treated me well, and I was comfortable being alone.

I needed downtime, and there, I totally got away from business.

I was mindless of things needing to be done, but I also knew on Monday I would do it all.

Before long, I knew several of the staff at the casino. They invited me to parties, so I met a lot of people. I won and lost like most gamblers.

On a trip to Atlantic City on a Friday afternoon, I was excited to get away for the weekend—away from business, which I loved and never tired of doing, but I did need a break. I was driving down, listening to music in a world all my own.

All of a sudden, on the expressway that was teeming with traffic, I saw a young man running for his life, zig-zagging across traffic. Now this was hilarious, because no doubt, he had been where he should not have been. He was in undershorts and carrying his shoes. This was in the pinelands, and there were pine needles everywhere. Can you imagine what they were doing to his bare feet?

There was a large row of houses from the direction he had run from. Otherwise, there was just a lot of vacant land. He must have had to walk a long way, and I do not think he had a cell phone with him.

I laughed so hard as I wondered how he was going to explain when he got home and was asked where his suit was. Then how was the woman going to explain the car in her driveway?

I have a great imagination, but could anyone doubt that scene?

I have told the story many times and still laugh hard each time. I would love to hear the end of his story, but with my imagination, it may be more fun telling it my way.

I got a call from John Phillips at Radio City Music Hall, whom I did not know. He said he would like for me to give a quote on labor for moves into and out of shows. This was a surprise to me as to how he picked me for this job. Needless to say, it was a prize account.

I said, "How soon would you like to make an appointment?"

He asked, "How soon can you make it?"

I said, "Well, I am about fifteen minutes away, but I need to put figures together."

I went and met him. What a nice person. He told me that Erie

Trucking had done the work but could not make payroll. Erie had suggested he call me.

I gave him the figures, and he said, "It's yours."

I said, "When do we start?"

He said, "Tomorrow morning."

I walked out saying to myself, "Nadine, you must have made a mistake on the figures. That was too easy." But, no, they were right.

That was a wonderful relationship, and it worked for many years, and then Madison Square Garden bought them out. But it was great working with him and the others in his office.

Sandy and Cherie Becker, who lived in the same building as I, went to Hawaii every year for a couple of months. For about a year, they started on me to come for a week or so. Finally, I said yes. So I made a reservation in the top hotel for New Year's and took my golf bag. They didn't play, but that was fine. I did not like to sit in the sun and do nothing, so that worked for me. When I got there, and it rained two days in a row.

On the third day, I decided to play even though it was misty. I was put with a Chinese gentleman and his young son. After a few holes, I could see this poor man was really not a good golfer. And there I was waiting on them all the time. I know he was embarrassed in front of his young son, so I quit.

It was not fun with the rain, anyway. That night at dinner, I said, "Well, guys, guess what?"

They burst out laughing and said, "Don't tell us. We

have already guessed. You are going to get out of here. Where are you going?"

I said, "Either to my condo in Saint Croix, Florida to visit friends, or to Vegas. But I really hear Vegas calling."

I got reservations, and when I landed in California to change planes, I called Vegas and could get into the Sands but only for two days. A big convention was coming. I said, "I will take the two days."

I checked in and started to play. I could not win anything, and it was fifty degrees.

I had summer clothes, of course, for Hawaii. The next morning, I decided to go to the Desert Inn, so I put on three layers of clothes and walked out and down there. As I was walking to the hotel, I looked up to the stars and said, "Bud, this trip is turning into a disaster. You'd better take me to a good machine."

Do not ask me how it happened, but I did not look at a machine in the front. I just went to the back to a small room, sat down at a dollar machine, and started to play. I took $200 out and was testing, when this machine was paying every time I pulled the handle. I started putting into the machine next to me. Same thing.

I would fill up the trays, and they would come take them and cash them in for me. I started at ten in the morning, and I skipped lunch and kept playing. It was crazy, and I did not stop. At about 9:00 p.m., I hit for $10,000. The slots manager came over and took all my information and said, "You have been playing for hours without a break. Would you like to go have dinner? We will hold the machines."

I said, "I have never had a run like this. I will just keep playing." He asked me where I was staying. I told him and said, "But I have to be out tomorrow. They are sold out."

He said, "Well, you can stay here." Sure, they wanted their money back. He said, "We will take you back to your hotel tonight when you are ready to go and will pick you up in the morning to come here. You are carrying a lot and people have been watching and talking about your luck. Just go to special services when you are ready to leave. When you are here, pay for nothing. Put it on your room, and we will see how much we can give you. Let us get you something to eat."

So I said, "Okay."

He brought me a menu from the steak restaurant, and I thought, *Well, they do not mean a hot dog.* I ordered a steak, a baked potato, a salad, and a glass of wine.

I had never before or have I since seen what happened. A waiter arrived pushing a small table, white tablecloth and all. Behind him was another waiter pushing a chair right up to the machines. I thought, *And none of my friends are here to share with me.*

I quit at 1:00 a.m. and was driven back to the hotel. I threw all the cash on the bed. I had $5,000 in hundred-dollar bills, and I had a $10,000 check. I hid the cash under my pillow and decided to take the check home and have a ball with the rest.

I did all the things I normally would—getting a massage, getting my hair and nails done, and eating well. When I left, they only charged me taxes. I did spend the $5,000, but so what? I had a good vacation.

I said, "Thank you, Bud. I was not asking for that much."

I began to be lucky, and it became fun. It was like I could not lose for almost four years.

One trip soon after, I took my daughter, Mary, with me to Atlantic City, and we started playing a row of about five five-dollar machines at Bally's that I played a lot and had been very lucky with.

Now we were laughing and winning like crazy. She would hit for $500 or $1,000. Then we would hit sometimes hit three or four machines at a time.

Then I hit the $25,000 jackpot. Of course, with that, they took our picture together with our arms in a V over the winning numbers—three sevens. The picture hung on the wall at Bally's for three or four years. Mary took about $7,000 home with her. That was some run we had, and it was lots of fun.

After my trip to Hawaii, that same winter when we had the worst weather in the entire country, I decide in late January or early February to go to a warm climate to get away from the weather. I could not get reservations anywhere, as everyone was going for better weather.

I knew there were three early flights to Saint Croix, so I decided to go to the airport to try for the first flight. I figured it was so bad that someone would not make it in because of weather. Sure enough, I got on. People were lying all over the airport because of canceled flights.

When I got to Puerto Rico, there was a big problem. There were people all over the floors there, and I did not have a reservation to get on the puddle jumper to Saint Croix. I went through three standbys with no luck, and I knew they did not fly those at night, so I decide to go to the Hilton in San Juan for the night. I had no bags.

I went in, and I walked straight to the casino, which Bud and I had been to several times. Everyone was still on the beach, so the casino was empty. I went into a small room with slots and started playing a one-dollar machine. My luck still held from early January. Within five minutes, I hit $10,000.

I will never forget a fellow working the casino who came over as the bells were ringing and said, "Do you know what you just did?"

I said, "Yes. I won the jackpot."

He said, "No one ever wins it."

I said, "I know. I have played here, and no ever does, but I just did."

He said, "I have to get the slots manager."

I nodded. Shortly, the manager came over and he said, "It will take a lot of time for us to count that much cash."

I told him I wanted a check, and he had the nerve to say, "We do not give checks."

I said, "Listen, I gamble, and I know casino commission rules. If I want a check, you have to give it to me."

One thing I knew is that you did not carry that much cash on you anywhere.

He said, "Okay, but it will take time."

I said, "I am here and will be staying tonight."

When he brought the check, I stopped playing and went to the desk for a room.

I asked the girl if they could copy something for me and said that I needed a postage-stamped envelope. I addressed it to my daughter, put a copy of the check in, and said in a note, "If anything happens to me, take this copy to the accountant or lawyer. They will know what to do." She got a big laugh, and I got to Saint Croix the next day.

Now with my luck that way, I kept going to Atlantic City, and it kept holding, so in the Champagne Room at

Bally's, I played the same machines all the time, and the jackpot got up to $76,000, and I called to see if anyone had hit it. No one had, so I went to play, knowing it was going to hit very soon. I arrived Friday afternoon, and I played all five machines that the jackpot covered. I played all night and all day, putting out very little money, and then into Sunday morning until 3:00 a.m.

I asked them to close the machines for me to rest a few hours, which they did. I went back down around 7:00 a.m. on Sunday and continued playing; it was very quiet as usual. People play late and sleep in on Sunday.

A woman started to bother me, saying, "You cannot play all these machines." I told her that there were the same machines all around that she could play. She kept on, and I ignored her, but I was tired, and after a half hour, I said, "Oh, take the one on the end." I knew the minute I did it that it would hit, and it did—within less than five minutes.

Word traveled fast that the blonde finally hit the jackpot, and some of the workers came running back to congratulate me. When I said it was not me, they were appalled and asked what I meant. I told them the story.

They all knew me, and one actually cried. She said, "You were supposed to win. Why did you not hit her or scream at her?"

I said, "No, it was not to be."

She said, "Why are you so calm?"

I said. "Life is funny sometimes; you do not get what you want."

Everyone at Bally's talked about it for a long time.

With that, my luck changed; I went for some time without winning, so I stopped while I was way ahead. I still gamble, but not heavily.

Betty Bumpers had tried for some time to get me to join the board of her foundation, Peace Links. I decided it was time for me to start being involved. I had a full plate with running Budd Enterprises, but I got comfortable with leaving for a meeting every once in a while in Washington. What a great group of intelligent women I met when I went down to Washington! They were all wives of members of the Senate or House of Representatives, except one lawyer from Boston. I was the only businesswoman.

That was a very interesting meeting, as it was held in the Bumpers' home in Bethesda, Maryland. I arrived and met everyone, and we talked for a while, and they asked me to go into another room while they voted on whether I should be a member of the board. Well, I had been asked to come by Betty Bumpers, so I figured it would not be a wasted trip, and indeed, I was invited to join.

The meeting started, and it got into the talk of their funds and what they were making on it. As a businessperson and having always done my own investments, I was taken aback by what they were getting in returns. I questioned their strategy. I explained how they could invest in perfectly safe things that would bring much more in dividends. They decided immediately that we should have a finance committee, and you know who they picked to help on it? No, I am not shy, but why be on a board if you are not going to be part of discussions and have input?

I enjoyed riding down on the train for meetings and usually stayed overnight with Dale and Betty. This gave me a break from business in my office by taking the train there and back. I sorted out many issues, as I usually did not get into conversations, so I could think without interruptions.

I was very aware of the fears in America, and many cities had bomb shelters in neighborhoods. I remembered that Chelsea Warehouse's main office at 216 East Forty-Seventh in New York City was one. The government put a Bomb Shelter sign on the building and gave supplies to be held in case of attack. They were in there for many years, and we finally threw them out years later and took down the sign. I was not there when they were put in. I wish I had not asked for them to be taken down. It's surprising that I would ask, as I am a collector, and they would be great collector items now.

Dale and Betty's children were so scared in the early

days of our problems with Russia and the so-called Cold War, and they talked to Betty about it. As she listened, she decided to do something because of their fears. That's when she formed Peace Links, which was an organization of women who would go around the world to talk to women working in government offices. The idea was for women with power to join us to work on the common goal of eradicating war and to try to convince the world to work together on this beautiful earth. Wars destroy and many times solve nothing.

Men have always been the warriors. Betty traveled to Russia and other countries when even our presidents did not. She had done a wonderful program in Arkansas getting all children immunized before the age of six when she was First Lady of Arkansas. (She and Rosalynn Carter became friends as the wives of governors. Rosalynn became involved as First Lady, and they carried forward with a federal program.) Betty made many contributions to the state of Arkansas as First Lady.

Betty is one of those women who grew up as I did, although Betty's father was a rancher who had lots of land, and they were considered rich, while we were not. Betty's father could also curse like no one else. Her life was quite different from mine, but as the years went by, we had lots in common. She did not curse except on occasion, but she is as colorful as anyone you will meet. She does not mince words on any subject. Do you think maybe we have a lot in common? One difference is that I cannot curse.

Many of the people reading this book do not realize the impact of the Cold War with Russia. We were all petrified. We were told they could blow us off the face of the earth. Children were taught how to get under their desks at school to protect themselves. How ridiculous. But parents did not protest, as they did not know what else to do.

Realizing that we were making a difference, we traveled extensively, and if I tried to name all the places we visited, I would still miss some, but to provide an idea, we went to The Hague for a peace conference. We spent a week in conferences, and it was very enlightening. We also went to East and West Germany, going through the Brandenburg Gate and seeing the drastic difference in how the people still lived as if time had stood still all the years after on the other side of the gate.

Our group went to so many places, but Budapest and Prague stand out. I love old architecture; it holds my attention greatly and always has. Why, I do not know, but give me anything old. I love the feel and the look of something that has been used and admired enough to survive the throwaway attitude of so many people—more so with Americans than any other group, especially since our country is so young to start with. If there is any truth that we have lived other lives, I must have at one time lived in a very old building or castle. My home reflects what I say.

In these travels, this part of a trip stands out. We arrived in Budapest, and we had an afternoon off. We could go to a museum, go for a massage, or make some other choice. I had invited Phyllis O'Donnell, wife of Tom O'Donnell, to go along. She and I decided on a massage. Of course, we felt we could go to many museums in New York.

We arrived at a huge building that no doubt in the years before their devastating wars was magnificent hotel, but now it was like an old, elegant woman who had not aged well. We went into the women's area after walking through the lobby with men walking with just towels on. We met with a woman we later called Nurse Ratched from that wonderful movie with Jack Nicholson, *One Flew Over the Cuckoo's Nest*. She spoke little English, but we made her understand that we were there for massages. She handed each of us one small piece of cloth—like a twin bedsheet but smaller, and then she led us to a small stall-like structure made of chicken wire with a shower just big enough for us to stand together butt to butt.

We removed our clothes and showered. Phyllis and I have known each other for years, and I grew up with six sisters, so this was no problem. Still, we were trying hard not to laugh. After all, we were in a country that was totally different from ours, and we were guests.

We dried ourselves off with our cloth wrap and put it back around our bodies, and she led us into a room for our massages. Of course, the cloths were wet and sticking to our bodies.

We went into an open room with about six tables with these huge Russian women getting massages. Over each table was a lightbulb hanging just on the electric wire. The staff did not speak English, but it only took a second for us to know that there had been a buzz about two American women who were coming in. First of all, to them, we must have looked starved. There was no wondering of the reason for their laughter.

You had to see it to know what we were in for. The tables were very old—just metal tables that, in our country, might be used as workbenches. They each had a rubber mat that was yellow, very grained, and hard, and they used a regular water hose like we use in the yard to put water on us, along with a bucket of water and a bar of soap to vigorously rub the soapsuds on.

I was called first. Off came the sheet that was by then melded to my body. I was used to soft lights and music, but the bare lightbulb was just above my eyes, and instead of a soothing massage, my body was being scrubbed like I had never bathed before. Not only that, but they were all talking and laughing. I knew it was me, the skinny American, at whom they were laughing.

I heard Nurse Ratched taking Phyllis over for hers. Phyllis is funny beyond words, and I knew we were going to laugh the rest of our lives and tell the story many times.

That night, we were going down to dinner in the little hotel in which we were staying. I had the bright idea that Phyllis and I should dress a little elegantly and tie all our purchases from the trip around our bodies. We looked like a walking flea market—tin tea cans, scarves, jacket, and a beautiful black chiffon skirt with black shorts underneath. We had been on a shopping spree. We waited until we were sure everyone would be there.

As usual, Phyllis and I were going to find some way to laugh. Everyone did laugh so hard, and cameras clicked, and we asked them how the museums were. They wanted to know about our afternoon, and we told them in great detail. We were a bunch of women very dedicated to our cause, but we managed to have a lot of humor mixed in.

We kind of sat in some order on the bus—some were rowdy in the front, and others who wanted to rest were in the back. You know where I sat.

The next trip that stands out is our mission to

Cuba—it took a whole year to be cleared. We flew to Florida on a commercial flight and then took a private air service to Cuba. We were all excited.

We had all meetings arranged in advance. Our first meeting was with Raul Castro's wife, who held a government job very high up. We went into a beautiful home with artwork beyond words. Of course, it had belonged to someone of great wealth but had been confiscated by the brothers.

When we walked in, we were greeted through an interpreter.

After introductions, Mrs. Castro accused us as being part of the government officials who did not respect Cuba. I was sitting next to Betty, getting madder by the minute and wondering why Betty was not interrupting her to get the respect we deserved.

Betty let Mrs. Castro blow off steam and then said in a very calm voice, "Mrs. Castro, have you not been advised we are a peace group? We do not come here as representatives of the United States government. We came here to learn from you what we can do to help your people and to let you know that there are people like us who care about Cuba and her people. We want to help bridge that misunderstanding."

All of a sudden, this woman who was not supposed to

understand English smiled and then spoke perfect English, and the rest of the meeting was very pleasant. When it was over, we got hugged and kissed, and we took many pictures with her. She was tall, big, and very elegant.

Mrs. Castro later died, and Raul was in charge since Fidel's health issues had become too large for him to continue his rule. We never knew she and Raul were divorced. It was reported in our newspapers when she died. She told us how she and the women had carried the guns out of the mountains in the overthrow of Batista. They were not suspected, and they carried them under long dresses to hand to Fidel's men.

Some newscaster was recently laughing about Fidel having to ride around in '50s cars. Let me tell you, they are magnificent and would go for tremendous amounts by collectors. They made the parts by hand, and the paint jobs would put any in the United States to shame.

I certainly do not condone in any way what has happened to Cuba. I found the people beautiful but felt such sorrow that such a country and the people have lived in poverty for so long, and our government has never tried to have real dialogue until now.

We met with heads of schools and hospitals and visited a pharmaceutical company. The school was especially touching to me. When we arrived, the first graders were in the school yard. They met us, and to our amazement, they were playing with a blood pressure cuff that was from the '50s. It was a mess, but they all wanted to be doctors, so they wanted to take our blood pressures. They had a wooden crate that Betty sat right down on or pretended to be sitting on—actually, she was squatting down over the crate. They put it on her arm.

The little doctor shook his head. This other little guy came over with a stick to put in her mouth to look at the tongue. I couldn't believe that Betty opened her mouth like nothing strange was happening and let them put the stick in her mouth. I knew I was next.

Well, thank God I passed their test in their minds. I did not have to take the tongue test. I might have gagged.

Then we went into the school and visited several classes, and then we went on to one with older students. All of a sudden, I saw about six using old Braille machines. I stayed behind with them. You already know about my family with blindness. I went over, bent down, and told them about my own experience with blindness in the family. I told them how my father always took his hands to my face and felt it and traced each feature and told me I was beautiful. I took my hands to each of their faces and traced theirs. I do not think anyone had ever told them how they looked. I told them the color of their eyes and so on. The smiles on their faces were worth a million dollars to me.

Then I found that they could use the machine for one sentence a day, as they did not have paper. I talked to their teacher and found out that the paper came from California. I got the name of the company, and I called them when I got back to New York and asked if they could donate and send paper to a Cuban school. The person said, "We cannot donate to everyone who needs."

So I said, "If I donate half, will you match?"

She said, "Yes."

Little did I know what I would go through when it was delivered to me in New York. The teacher had said I could give it to the Cuban embassy on Lexington Avenue in New York, so I went down and walked in, and it was like the 1950s. The telephone sitting on a table was an old rotary phone, and a young man in a pale-blue polyester suit that was also from the 1950s was in charge.

I told him that I wanted to bring school supplies down to send by embassy mail pouch. He told me that they did not send anything back to Cuba. At first, I was speechless, and then I asked him if he knew of any way to get the paper to the kids. He told me that there was a man on Twenty-Third Street who shipped by boat when he had the opportunity. He gave me a telephone number. I talked to a man who said he could take the paper but had no idea when it would be delivered.

I took a taxi, as the paper was really heavy, and I told the driver to help me to the door. What I did not realize was that the office was upstairs about fifty steps. By the time I realized this, the driver had already left, so I left it and ran upstairs. A very elderly man was there by himself.

I said, "Do you have anyone who can help? I have the very heavy paper I talked to you about."

He said, "I will help you." He had things stacked to the ceiling. I left them. I have always prayed those poor children got the paper. Why did I not use my Teamsters? They were always willing to help with donations.

We had visited Hemingway's hangout, and it was still the same as when he was there; it was a very small place with lots of old pictures and signatures on the walls.

We saw people standing in line on Sunday patiently waiting for two hours to get an ice cream cone.

There were buses where everyone stood, coming in from the countryside all crammed in together, and I am talking about seventy-five to one hundred on a bus.

We also went to the National Hotel of Cuba, where all the stars and Mafia went as well lots of others, including Bud. He had gone there with a cousin, George Vario, just before the revolution. He had told me they had heard the shooting up in the mountains. He thought it funny that he almost got caught in a war. He said they almost got caught in downtown Havana.

I just recently was buying trucks from a Cuban who came to this country during the revolution. When I told him about Bud being at the hotel and hearing the shooting up in the mountains, he told me that they did not fight up in the mountains and that what Bud and his cousin had heard were shots just down from the hotel where they lined men up against a cement wall and shot them only a short distance away.

It looked the same as at the overthrow of the island. There were photos of the stars of the day everywhere, and the hotel and everything was beautiful. There were no Cubans there except workers.

Our hotel was very new looking, and it had good food. No Cubans except help were allowed in. Our bellmen were all doctors or lawyers who could make cash money as tips. Hopefully, they got to keep it, because we all tipped as if we were in an American hotel. The government controlled pay, and it was the equivalent of twenty dollars per month in any job. How sad to see these proud people reduced to living under the Castro rule.

We learned that all people were required to go to the doctor once a month. It sounded like good medicine, but that was not so; each square block had a monitor to keep records, and it was really a means of keeping track of the people.

I had an experience at the hospital that was hard to accept. I had been to a dinner a few nights before leaving at the Columbus Club, an Italian club where everyone was very giving of time and money. A heart specialist there was going to Cuba the following week that I was to go, and we talked about our trips. He was a speaker that night at the club and told of how he was going to operate on a young girl in Cuba who would not survive without his going.

We were in this very hospital in Cuba, and I had not even thought about it when he was telling about his upcoming trip.

Our Cuban guide told us about the patients and mentioned that a little girl was to have an operation by an American doctor. She took us to where the children were, and they were in beds from the 1940s—metal and painted white. Needless to say, it was lead paint, and it was all chipped. Then she said, "The doctor is coming to do an operation on this little girl."

I said, "I met the doctor just a few days ago."

Then she said, "Can you get hold of him?"

I said, "Maybe, through a friend of mine."

She told me that one piece of rubber tubing was broken and that she wanted him to bring a replacement with him.

I called Sandra Methlie-Rossano, my friend who had invited me as guest to the club that night, and told her. She called me back and said that he could not bring the piece because our government required a list of any items being brought into Cuba a year in advance. That was how long it took us to get papers to go to Cuba. It took him that long too.

When the doctor heard a piece was broken, he did not make the trip, as the operation would not have been successful, and it would be the fault of an American doctor as would be played by Fidel and company. I felt so bad. It was just a stupid tubing piece, and the doctor was not allowed by our country to bring it with him.

Well, at least that was one of the reasons we were there. We would try to convince our government when we came back that we needed change—not for Fidel but for the people of Cuba.

We also learned that almost every country had built a hotel way out. Cuba had one far outside of Havana. The hotel gave a portion of its income to the Cuban government, so I was told.

The United States, ninety miles away, could not arrange this tiny rubber tube to save a child's life. Why do the American people not demand the change since we let people come from all over the world travel here and us to go freely to other countries?

I met another interesting person going to Washington, DC, by train some years later again with Peace Links. I would usually take my *Wall Street Journal* and the *New York Times* with me and read until about Baltimore. There was a young fellow sitting next to me quietly. When I put my papers down, he asked me if I knew Washington, DC, and I said yes.

We introduced ourselves—Dan Brown and Nadine Schramm. I asked what he did, and he said that he was a writer. It seems so many times when people do nothing, they tend to say they write. I then asked what he wrote, and he replied that he wrote fiction.

"Have you been published?"

"Yes," he said. Then he asked me what I did. Well, he may not have believed me when I told him that I was a trucker, but we had a good conversation.

Then he asked me if he should take the metro or a cab to his hotel. I asked which one he was staying in, and he told me. I said, "Listen, I am going by taxi, and I can easily drop you off."

Transportation was not so easy in Washington because there were not many buses.

He was happy since it was his first time there. He was going to a literary meeting, and I was going to a party honoring either Betty or Dale. It was supposed to snow that night, and we each wished each to have a good meeting.

I asked about the title of his book, and he told me that one was

Angels & Demons. Although I read a lot and all kinds, I did not know his works. He said, "Give me your address; I will send you one."

I got it and could not put it down and wrote him a thank-you note saying, "You cost me a night's sleep; I loved it."

When his book *The Da Vinci Code* came out, he had a book signing at Barnes & Noble. I went and was amazed to see so many people, but I should have known. He was great with his description of how he researched the book. He and his wife spent six months in the Vatican in areas in which no outsider had ever been allowed. It was very intriguing.

I walked up in line to have two books signed. I said, "You will not remember me."

He looked up and said, "A snowy night in Washington, DC." Inside the book, he wrote,

> To Nadine,
> With fond memories of a snowy night in Washington
>
> —Dan Brown

I laughed and said, "I cannot wait to show all my girlfriends; they are going to be very jealous."

He asked me to wait until he was finished signing. He wanted to introduce me to his wife, a lovely woman. I told him, "I hope to have my trucks in the movie when it is made."

He said, "I will never let them do a movie."

I said, "Money talks." You know what happened—it was made into a great movie.

I keep thinking with his new book, which is all about the secret codes of Washington, DC, and when I met him, he did not know the city. He sure learned it better than anyone and in a very short time frame.

CHAPTER 14

Special times with Family

I have traveled with each of my three grandchildren, as I gave all of them for their high school graduation gift a trip wherever they wanted to go—a trip to Rome, a trip to Spain, and an Alaskan cruise. I went on these trips with them.

Michael's was to Alaska on a cruise ship, and he was wide eyed and loved traveling. It was so much fun to see his excitement. We also spent time in Seattle where we had a lot of fun shopping and sightseeing.

I took my daughter with us but not the two granddaughters. I realized it should just be their trips with Grandma. He still loves to travel and has traveled to many places; he just jumps on a flight to anywhere in the world by himself.

I took Amanda on a trip to Spain. My hairdresser and friend Judy Serringer, and her husband, Robert, had bought a house there and kept asking me to visit, so I decided it would be a good place to take Amanda on her gift trip.

Their home was way up in the mountains along very windy roads in beautiful country. We had so much fun, and Amanda loved it. They have a son, and although he was older, they told him he was to take Amanda places in the evening after our dinners for her to see how the locals lived. Well, I can tell you those kids know how to party.

We had late dinners, as they all eat late there. We would leave them, but without a car, he had to call his parents when they were ready to come home. The reason for them not to have the car was that the roads were especially dangerous after they had been drinking. Sure enough, the calls came at two or three in the morning, and down we went to pick them up.

They had laughed and told me not to worry about Amanda being with an older boy, as they had given him strict orders; Amanda was Nadine's granddaughter and thus was to be treated with great respect. It was funny, because he had known me since he was two years old. Well, she had a ball. I could not have chosen a better place.

I had to think of a special place to take Kelly too. She chose Rome. I was very excited with the choice. It was very interesting; when we got there, she had a map and had already picked a lot of places she wanted to see. I am not good with maps of cities, but I did not have to be; she had everything planned, and we were all over Rome and on side trips. It is a beautiful city, and we had so much fun there.

I must say these trips with my grandchildren are great memories, and I got to know each of them so much better being alone with them for a week at a time.

There were a few things that I did with Ralph at different venues. When we were in Chicago, we were invited at the convention to go out on an FBI boat in the harbor. We were not supposed to be on it, but we were having a good time. Ralph, as you already know, was very active in the Democratic Party of Arkansas. He was recognized everywhere we went, it seemed.

I had on one of my captain hats.

One of the FBI agents asked me, "Are you a sailor?"

"Yes, I am." They turned the wheel over to me.

At about that time, we saw a boat in distress, so we had to go below. They pulled over, and thank goodness the people got their boat started. We would not have been in good shape towing them back to shore.

One of the parties I liked so much was called the Blue Jean Bash. This party was in Washington, DC. Ralph was all excited, but I never wear jeans, so it was time to go shopping for some. I found the jeans and then said,

"Ralph, I cannot wear a cowboy shirt; for some reason, it does not fit my style."

We walked down the street, and I saw a beautiful beaded jacket that was black, red, and white in the window. I said, "Let's go in." I tried it on and said, "This is it."

I was the most photographed at the party. Dare to be different.

My snorkeling experience on Buck Island was a big step for me. I have stated that I am not a swimmer, but I was down for a week in Saint Croix with my friend Phyllis O'Donnell after Bud passed away. She needed a break from home. Her daughter had triplets, and she had been a major help taking care of them. She said there was no sleep; when one got quiet, another started to cry. She told me how many diapers were used every day, and it seemed enough to keep one busy just with that job of changing. Now she could do anything and was not afraid, so I took her to Buck Island by the operator's open passenger boat. All the way out, the guide was talking to everyone and telling them what to expect.

He came over to me, and I said, "I am not snorkeling, because I do not swim well. Also this is in the ocean."

He weighed about 125 pounds, and he told me that he would take care of me and to not worry. At first I said yes, and then I said no. I thought about it and continued to waffle back and forth.

When we got there, he said, "I will put a tube for you to hold on to, and I will pull you." I agreed and then found that another young lady was going to be pulled by him too.

The way I looked at it was if she panicked, he would have to leave me, and if I panicked, he would leave her. I decided to take my chances, as everyone who had ever done it said it was a wonderful experience. Bud had gone several times, but this was after he passed, so my real protector was not with me. Phyllis had made me feel comfortable, and I could not let her best me. She was such a trooper on all the escapades. If I did not do it too, how could we talk about it later on in our lives?

I am so happy I did it, as it is one of the wonders of our magnificent universe. We started out, and at first, I was nervous, but then the wonders of the underwater sights took complete control of me. I had never seen anything like it. He had told us that it would look like we were one or two feet above all the coral, but it might be as much as twenty feet below us. He warned us to be aware that at some points we would be close and to stay in formation, as the coral would cut badly.

When we finished, I was fine, but my little partner was sick to her stomach in the back of the boat. I got her a Coke and talked to her, and she said she was embarrassed. I said, "Do not be; I was the one being pulled along with you. I thought I would be the one sitting here."

Another time, I took a girlfriend with me to Saint Croix, and she wanted to learn to play golf, so she took some lessons but was just riding in the cart on this particular day. We went to Carambola Golf Resort where we always played if we did not play at the Buccaneer. I was a very good golfer at that time, and the starter and manager knew me. A group of men who played there every day of the year were getting ready to tee off. There were seven of them, as one of their group was a no-show.

It was a busy course that day, and the starter put me with these two groups. I think he may have been thinking I might take them—or if not, I would give them a good run.

I sometimes played with a fellow who was one of the top players in the Caribbean, so they knew I could hold my own. I was a woman, and you could feel and see their disdain.

I introduced myself, and off we went. I am beyond competitive on any given day, but now I wanted to prove a point that there were good women golfers. They always played for money, so they were serious players. They said with disparagement that they bet every hole and that I would probably not want to.

I said, "Well, I'm a sport, so put me in."

The worst thing for any golfer is to be mad or upset, and they were both. On the first hole, two flubbed badly, and the other did not do so well, either.

We pulled down to the ladies' tee, and I blasted away straight down and a good distance. This made it even worse for them. I parred at the first hole. I was already intimidating for these guys. Danielle was laughing, and I had to shush her. She was keeping my score, but so were they. I had no idea what the other four in front of us were doing, but we were having to wait for them to finish holes.

This kept going on, and I was having one of my best games ever. I was parring and even had a couple of birdies. Well, after we had played the eighteenth, we went into the bar area. I knew I had beaten most of them, but I was not sure if I had beaten all of them because I did not have their scores.

Then the bar was alive. Word had traveled throughout the club.

They went to a table to count the scores, and Danielle and I sat at the bar as they were counting. She kept going over to see the count and kept coming back to tell me the scores on each hole. She said, "Nadine, you are beating them on every hole."

The pro and starter came in, and then others came. The word traveled Nadine had beaten the a——— off them, and she was in on the bets. A lot of guys did not like this group, as they would not let anyone play with them; they thought they owned the course.

I won most holes.

I tried to send them a drink at that point, but they would not accept. No woman could pay for drinks. I think it was more because too many people would know I had beaten them.

They did not offer to buy for us. The bartender poured a drink for us, leaned over, and said, "This is on them; they just don't know it."

They had to pay me most all the winnings. I offered them the chance to win it all back the next day. They did not take me up on it. Any time after that, I would get a little cheer from everyone. It was fun, but I felt bad, as I am not one to emasculate a man. I know the difference between men and women, and I like my femininity.

Ralph and I were both invited to Washington for Betty and Dale Bumpers' daughter's wedding. Ralph did not go, but I did; that was unusual, as no one loves a party more than he does.

This was about three months after the Clintons were in office. It was a lovely wedding, and when I turned to see Brooke coming up the aisle, I realized that President Clinton, First Lady Hillary, and Chelsea were sitting behind me. I was sitting with some of the Bumpers family.

That, of course, was the last time that happened. It was a lovely service, and then it was on to the reception. There were only about one hundred people, and what struck me funny was that there was no security check with the president being there. I am sure they must have been in the background, but I sure never saw them.

Everyone there was well known to one another. Most had been vetted for the White House visitations during the inauguration.

Some cousins of the Bumpers were there that I had not seen in many years. They were asking what I was doing. I told them about the trucking. I was asked, "Nadine, how can you run a trucking company? Is it not hard for a woman?"

I told them that I loved it and that the men all accepted me. I laughed and said after plowing and picking cotton, anything was a piece of cake. I reminded them that I had always done a man's work. What a lovely time—one I treasure very much.

Joan Baldridge, who had worked with Bill Clinton when he was governor and also when he was in Washington as well as with Madeline Albright, asked me to go to Saint Petersburg, Russia, for the first exhibit of all the paintings retrieved from Germany after World War II. They had been stored in the basement of the State Hermitage Museum and had been brought out cleaned and now for showing the world. The State Hermitage Museum is beautiful, and the paintings are magnificent. They also had furniture, which I of course was very interested in. It was a very nice trip, and we had lots of laughs.

We hired a driver and guide, and we needed them. We tried to do a lot, and we did see so much. The hotel was new and fine, but the food was terrible. We drank a lot champagne, and I loved the smoked salmon, but that was all either of us enjoyed.

We went to one of the finest restaurants and took our guide in with us to eat. She was very upset with what we saw. There was a table of maybe twenty young Russians at a huge, long table. The young women were beautiful. It was filled with about twenty-five bottles of liquor. Think in terms of deception of reality in Russia. The women and men were dressed in the latest fashion—I mean over-the-top pricewise. They were loud.

She whispered to us, saying, "Mob."

We wanted to bring back some caviar, so we went to the showplace store. They had no caviar. We tried everywhere, but there was none for sale. They told us to pick it up on the way to the airport. No luck. I finally found some in the airport in Finland.

We went on a tour, and I will never forget one scene. We were overlooking a small park that our guide told us was called the dancing park. I said, "How nice."

She said no—it was where they made the prisoners walk with bare feet on embedded nails turned up. How barbaric is that?

I had the privilege of meeting First Lady Rosalynn Carter. She and Betty Bumpers traveled to New York to visit a school in the Bronx. I had one of my teamster drivers, Vinnie Delellis, drive us up. We visited with the children, teachers, and many elderly ladies who were grandmothers of these very young students. Most did not speak English, and the schoolteachers were helping them to learn. They were the caretakers, as sometimes both parents had become addicts.

I was amazed how First Lady Rosalynn Carter got down on the floor and talked to these children. The elders told us they were learning English through music and the children.

I hope those children remember that day, as I remember so many of the things in my life at that age. What a treasure for them to have the First Lady and a senator's wife there with them. I trust people who relate to children. That day I thought how lucky I had been in my childhood—no drugs and all the family at the table for every meal. So many families I know do not have regular meal times in our hurried world of today. And then there are the parents who just walk away from responsibilities, leaving their children adrift.

Only in the last few years, my brother Ralph, who had been in construction and knew all the top people throughout Arkansas, called to tell me he had been to the capital in Little Rock. Of course, he had through the years spent lots of time there, so I was not surprised to hear he had been there.

He said a lot of people had asked for me.

I said, "Ralph, who asked?"

He said, "Oh, I do not remember their names."

I was shocked; he could always recall hundreds of names and then ask about wives, children, uncles, and more. I realized at that moment that he was dealing with the beginning of Alzheimer's disease.

There were the calls when he had driven fifty miles from home and did not know why he was there. My sister-in-law Nita was very good at handling the situation. She would tell him, "Do not move." She would send a member of the family to go get him. Then she had to take the keys, but he never resisted. His wife and children knew he should go to a nursing home for his sake.

I miss the person he was, but I loved the person he later became. He still had that big smile. I never saw him lose his temper. Like our mother and father, he always had a happy attitude, and all the personnel in the home loved him. It was sad to see him not recognize the ones dearest to him. He loved to walk, and he did long walks in the home. They drew arrows pointing him back to his room, and he would follow them even though he remembered little of anything else.

I shall always be in debt to him for all the years of being right in the middle of the main political scenes with Dale Bumpers' governor and senator campaigns and Bill Clinton's campaigns. I knew a lot of people there from being with him at political meetings and parties.

I had a laugh on my nephew Dr. Gene Shelby of Hot Springs, Arkansas, Ralph and Nita's son. He was having a party and dinner for about seventy of our family at his home during one of the family reunions. I said, "Gene, have you ever thought about what is going to happen to your yard in the future?"

"No, why?"

"Well, the way I see it, since President Clinton lived with his mother next door when he was a child, they will probably put the library on the property next door, and they will need your property for a parking lot."

Everyone laughed except him—and then he did too.

I lost Ralph in 2012. It is a big void, but he had lived a good long life. I shared so much with him through all the years, but I could not wish for him to live with the loss of his memory or without knowing even his children.

I have a friend who came to town to take me around for a couple of days. First we went to the Palace Hotel, one of the most elegant places in New York, and had one drink. He got quite a kick out of watching a parade of beautiful young women all looking like top models. However, no doubt they were ladies of the night—more commonly known as hookers.

They were easy to spot. They had one drink, and if there were no takers, they went on to the next place.

Then we went to the Plaza for dinner in the Oak Room and had another drink, but neither he nor I were into heavy drinking. We had a lovely dinner and started to leave. As always, I had on very high heels—my favorite green sandals, which were very comfortable.

I went out the door to go down about six steps covered with outdoor carpet, and on the first step, my heel caught on a piece of slightly torn carpet, and down I went. The doorman and my tall friend were both trying to catch up with me. I ended up at the bottom and jumped up.

Security arrived, and they made me go back inside to get information about who I was. They tried to get me to go to a hospital for a checkup, but I insisted that I was fine. I gave them my name, address, and telephone number.

The next morning, I got a call from security while I was sipping coffee and reading the *Times*.

"Mrs. Schramm, how are you?"

"I am fine."

"We would still like you to go to be checked out."

"No, I am fine."

They were worried about a lawsuit probably, and they called again the next day and got the same answer from me. Once they knew I was not going to sue, the man said to me, "We have watched the tape of your fall about a dozen times. We have laughed so hard and even made bets as to what you do—everything from a dancer to a trapeze artist and many other things. What do you do?"

"I am a trucker."

"No way!" he said. I hear that often.

I said, "So let me see the tape you are having so much fun with."

He said, "No, we cannot do that." I did not think it was fair.

I was passing by the Plaza a couple of days later as I was on my way to the New York Athletic Club. I stopped into the security office at the Plaza. I said, "Come on, guys, you have had so much fun. Let me see it." The answer was no.

They assured me they noticed that I did not tear my stockings and that not a hair was out of place. My skirt had not torn and never went up. They said I was up as if nothing had happened.

My date from that night sent me a package later, and inside I found a license plate—the same as regular New York State plates—reading BEST LEGS. No, I never put it on my car, but I do laugh when I look at it.

CHAPTER 15

Earning Honors, and Making New Friends along the Way

Jim Leavey, one of my most loyal teamsters, called me one afternoon and wanted me to come down to the Lower East Side to a bar for a drink. I questioned the location, and he assured me it was okay and also said that other teamsters would be there. They had just finished a pilot for the TV show *The Sopranos*, which my trucks were on. (The name meant nothing at the time.)

I went, and when I walked in, I saw a group of them, and they had a torn, fake-leather bar stool saved for me. It was not the kind of place they usually took me. They kept a seat next to me open, and in a short time, in came a big guy, and they seated him next to me.

He started talking to me in really rugged language. I thought, *What are my teamsters doing with this guy?*

I could tell Jim and the others were enjoying my discomfort, and I wondered why.

I stayed long enough not to be rude, trying hard not to disappoint Jim and the others. I had no idea of who the guy was, but I felt he was not someone I would want to spend time with, and I was kind of amazed that they had wanted me to meet him.

Well, that was some introduction to the great Tony of *The Sopranos*. It was the wrap party. He was so into the part that he could not walk away from it. What an actor! He gave many people lots of great television. His death was a great loss to the entertainment industry. Later, I so much appreciated the introduction and was in his company several times and have pictures of us at events. Out of character, he was very soft spoken.

The teamsters got a big kick out of my reaction, and Budd trucks were on the job all seasons.

My grandchildren were all doing well. Michael made good grades when he was in high school, and when he was sixteen, he worked at Boston Chicken, and they loved him. Then he went to Wheaton College and made good grades even while working at Starbucks thirty hours per week. He had worked at Starbucks in Westport, Connecticut, too.

Kelly was one of the top tennis players in the Northeast when she was very young. Also, she could not understand grading in her school when she was a first grader. She got all straight *A*s or *A*+s on her report card.

She called me and told me about her report card and said, "Grandma, they need to have something higher than A+ because some others got them, and I know I am smarter than them." It was said with such innocence, and I am afraid she was right. She got scholarships to different colleges for her tennis as well as grades.

I got a call from her while she was in her first year of college, and she told me she was staying up until midnight studying and then up at 4:00 a.m. for tennis practice, and she needed advice, as she knew she was going to burn out. She told me she had tried to talk to both her parents, and they could not give any advice.

I told her I would listen and try to help her, but first I told her she would have to make the final decision. I told her there was no doubt that she might be a top tennis player in the world, because she was that good, but she might have an injury that would end that career, and then what would she do?

So I said, "Kelly, you have a great brain that should be used, and you might develop something that would benefit millions of lives."

I did not have to say another thing. She said, "Grandma, thank you so much. I just needed for someone to validate what I was thinking."

She went to the University of Tennessee studying

biomedical engineering. She is now in Minneapolis working for one of the largest pharmaceutical companies in the world.

In 1999, Ralph came to visit me in New York. He had a mission.

General McArthur had been baptized in the Episcopal church in Little Rock where Ralph was very active as a deacon. He told me that he wanted to meet Mrs. Douglas McArthur. I knew she lived in the Waldorf Towers, so I walked him over and asked the concierge at the desk, who said, "Well, I can't let you talk to her, but I will give a note to her."

Ralph and I went back to my apartment only a couple of blocks away. We composed a note telling her about Ralph's wish to get a Bible signed by her to put in the little library of the church (they already had some items on the general).

The next morning, Ralph was reading the paper with a cup of coffee when the phone rang. A young woman on the line said that she was Mrs. McArthur's secretary and that she would like to speak to Ralph Shelby.

I went into my living and told him that Mrs. McArthur was on the line. He said, "Do not bullshit me."

I laughed and said, "She is on the line." Then he knew I was serious.

He talked to her, and she said she would be happy to see him, so he met her for lunch at the Waldorf Towers desk. Ralph asked if it was all right if he brought his sister who lived in the neighborhood, and she said yes. He asked if he would be able to take a picture, and she again agreed.

We went at noon as she had requested and walked up to the desk in the main dining room. At the desk, they asked us to stand aside because she was not there yet. I glanced around, and there was a beautiful lady sitting in a wheelchair with a caretaker, and she was no doubt giving us the once-over.

All of a sudden, over they came. She said, "Hello. You must be Mr. Shelby." Then she turned to me and asked my name, and I introduce myself, and we were taken to the dining room.

She was absolutely stunning. I will never forget that she had on a light orchid chiffon dress, and her hair and complexion were flawless. She was beautiful and very gracious. (She was 102 when she died only a couple of years later.) Ralph told her all about the church and showed her a copy of General McArthur's baptism certificate. She said he had never mentioned Arkansas but that no doubt he was there as a child.

We were both very excited. What an honor to be sitting with her. Ralph told her of being in the navy and on one of the ships besides witnessing General McArthur sign the armistice. She said, "I was there." She then told how she traveled with him all the time. Surprisingly, it included all his missions during World War II. We took pictures, and I have them, but the lighting was such that they came out very light. I wish we had taken a better camera.

She was most gracious, and the next day, I sent her a dozen red roses. She called and asked for me. She had asked for my number and had said, "We are neighbors; let's get together."

She said, "Are you the lovely lady who sent me flowers?"

I said yes and told her how much we appreciated her company and generosity. Again she said, "Let us get together." I thought she was just being pleasant.

A couple of years later, I read her obituary, and the funeral was to be private. At that moment, it dawned on me that she had outlived her friends. She had a son she never mentioned. I thought, *Nadine, you let her down. She needed a friend.*

Many years later, I decided to ask my nieces to come to New York to visit me. They came from all over the country. I had to make it special, so I called it "Aunt Nadine's Pajama Party." I said, "Bring your sexy pj's, and we will have a competition to see who has the best." We had a ball. Talk about being creative!

One morning, July 20, 2002, they wanted to go over to *The Today Show*—eight of them and me. They made signs with the name of the party. Of course, the crew came right over to us and wanted to know what it is all about before the show started, and they wanted to know which one was Aunt Nadine. They talked to us a bit. And I said, "Girls, we are going to be on the show. You'd better call husbands and family if you want them to see."

Sure enough, the show started, and we saw the crew coming back to us. They talked to me and wanted to know what the party was about all over again and on air.

By the time we got back to the apartment, the phone was ringing off the hook. First was Rick Schramm, who told me he was sitting on his patio reading the paper and having coffee with the television on when he heard the words *Aunt Nadine*, and he immediately knew it was me because there's only one Aunt Nadine. (There are others, I am sure, but not many.) At the time, he was working for me, and I had told him about the big party. I got calls from across the country, and so did they. I have the picture made by the studio photographer.

I got a request to cosponsor a day with President Bill Clinton at New York University, which I did. I took three people, and it was a miserable, windy, and rainy day. We did not get there until midmorning, and those in charge had not been informed that the couple who were cosponsors with me and I were to have breakfast with him, so I missed it.

Then came lunch, and they had boxed lunches, or we could go out again—and then we were told that my group was supposed to have lunch upstairs again with the president and special group.

Well, it all worked out, and it was very special. If any have not had the pleasure of hearing President Clinton speak in person, it is a memorable occasion. He never needs notes and can speak without a problem for two hours, keeping everyone's attention.

I treasure all those times.

Shortly after receiving my NYWA Award, I was asked to speak to approximately 137,000 students in three different groups at Miami Dade College. Of course, I had to say yes.

I did not go to college, and there I was being asked to speak at the largest college in the United States. I hoped my mom and dad were watching from heaven; they would have been proud. Again, I was the child who was not the best student in the family. I think of what my brothers and sisters could have contributed given the chance I had.

I did not know what was expected. I was informed that I would first meet the dean and some professors for coffee and breakfast. I totally love meeting people from all walks of life. I love young people, and I feel we owe the younger generation mentoring and encouragement to reach high and let them know that it takes hard work.

Sometimes, with today's fast-paced life, some have the feeling they are failing if they have not attained success by the age of twenty-five. I say work and gradually grow. Enjoy your friends and fellowship. You will grow old fast enough.

I was told a week or so in advance that I would first speak to a group of students for fifty minutes and then ten minutes of questions and answers from me. *That's a long time*, I thought—only to be told I would do that with three groups. Well, I was certainly not going to write a speech for it; I was just going to wing it.

My grandson, Mike, who is my big supporter, went with me. He had a part in my being asked; he had given a copy of my speech from NYWA to a professor.

During the first hour at Miami Dade, I was just so relaxed with the kids. I saw several of the professors who had been at the breakfast in the crowd. For fifty minutes, I told the students about my life and the many challenges I had faced, trying to make them realize that they would have many opportunities but needed to make choices and then work very hard to be successful. The students asked me for advice on the things they should expect and do going out into the business world.

One hour went so fast. No one walked out.

I realized how scary it must be today. Young people are asked to know what they want to do in life by the time they get out of high school. I never knew what I wanted to do; we just took jobs that we could find that paid a salary.

They asked me questions about how I started my first business and then ask how hard it was. I told them that getting what you really want is usually not easy. I just told them to choose what they loved and that if you do not love your work, I do not think you will ever be totally at your full potential. I also told them it takes a lot of hard work and determination.

Choose for yourself. This is your life. Never do what someone else chooses for you. Though suggestions of what they think you would be good at are fine, weigh them and then go with you own gut feeling.

Never use the word *can't*. Remember that you may try different things until you find one that you are truly happy getting up every morning for. When it feels like it's not work, you have hit bingo.

I walked to meet the second group of students with no rest in between. I looked up and saw two professors who had been at the last meeting. I asked, "What are you doing here? You were at the last one."

They laughed and said, "You did not use notes, so we know this will be totally different." It was.

I had been told that this group consisted of students who had not done well in high school and had realized that they needed that college degree. Now they were not only going to college but were working to pay for it. I was totally impressed, and I could relate to them. My parents could not really afford to send us to college, but they insisted that if any one of us chose to pursue higher education, they would somehow find a way. Not one of us did. There was such a need to go to work to help with the younger ones, and when one left home, there was one less farmhand, and the income would come down.

So I spoke to this group differently. I wanted them to understand that I had walked in similar shoes. But in my time, it was not so common for women to go to college. The feeling then was the boys should go and that the girls would marry one of them if lucky, but even most of the boys did not go because of the cost. College was very cheap by today's standards, but even $500 was out of reach for most, and unlike today, if you were not going to be a doctor or lawyer, the jobs available did not require higher education.

I knew this group came from families who did not have money to send them and that many were also from broken homes. I really wanted them to know I had never felt deprived but knew that I had to strive a little harder than some others.

When the questions came, I was astounded. I will never forget the first young man. The microphone did not work for them, so I told him to come down to me and that we would use the one on my lapel. He did, and I realized he was very nervous, so I took his hand, and I never turned loose. I was so proud of him that even though he was nervous, he still came down.

He asked, "How do I start a business?"

I asked, "What do you want to do?"

"I don't know."

I told him first pick out something he loved and then make a business plan and to not be afraid of failure, as fear causes defeat. I made sure he got a big cheer. No one else was coming down, so I said, "So what is wrong with you girls?"

Up stood a girl who looked like she was sixteen. She told me she was a single mother of a four-year-old with a crippling disease. She needed to be able to work from her home so she could take care of her baby. I asked her if she had any help from family members.

She said, "They do not understand." I looked at her

and thought that she was a young mother with a child; there was probably no father for the child, and she had been disowned. I may be wrong, and I hope so.

I asked if she had thoughts on what she might be able to do, and she said she was interested in gift baskets. I thought quickly and said, "Why do you not go to a florist in your area and ask them to teach you? They can bring the flowers to you and pick up arrangements. That way, you can take care of your son without leaving your home. Be honest with the people and your problem. The first, second, or third may not help you, but one will. I do truly believe there's always an angel if we only ask."

She said that it sounded like she could do it. I so badly wanted to help that young mother who was all alone with a handicapped baby. She must have had the baby when she was very young. Even for a couple it would be a very difficult undertaking, and there she was trying to get an education, work, and take care of a child.

Next up was a handsome young man full of swagger. He asked about the question of quitting school. His parents were telling him to get the education, and he wanted to quit and start his own business.

I said, "Listen to your parents; they are right. You are young; you have time to go into business. What do you want to do?"

He said, "I want to be a florist."

I called out to the professor, "Run and get that young lady who just left!" You should have seen that big tall professor run after my little girl. He came back with her.

I said to my future florist, "Meet your new partner. Buy the flowers, and she will make them into bouquets. Be partners. Now you both can do what you want. I want to hear how it works out. But at the same time, get the education."

I have not heard, but at least I gave them an option. I do hope for that young lady found something where she could be with her son. I still think of her often.

The final group of Miami Dade students were studying finance. It was a small group of maybe only twelve or fourteen, and it was a very interesting group. They were different; I could tell they worked together. Sure enough, they had won a contest against other schools. I enjoyed them, as I never studied finance but have always understood making money and keeping it.

If you do not have money, do not buy. Debt in many ways is taking this country on a trip I do not like.

Those students were smart, and I enjoyed talking with them. I felt the best advice I could give them was about going out into the business world where no doubt they would end up. I told them all to dress for success. If you do not have money for something nice, go to a resale shop, and for twenty dollars, you will come out with a business suit for your interview. Do not forget that you will also find the shoes in the same stores. First impressions last when you walk out that door.

When the meeting was over, their professor told me, "You just told them something that was such good advice that I could never say to them."

I left that college feeling like I had shared with them the knowledge that they surely were going to be just fine if I had come from my background and made it.

Those three hours went by very fast. I was not even hoarse. I treasure that time and was the receiver of a plaque as being a keynote speaker for Miami Dade School of Business Entrepreneurship Symposium. It has a special place in my office.

I have never been around guns, but my friend George Kalergios, owner of Tres Construction and assistant to District Attorney Robert Morgenthau, invited me to go to a range to practice shooting at a military range. I told him I had never shot a gun. He said, "Well, that is okay; we will have fun. Some others are going with us."

I met him on Forty-Second in front of a hotel, and another woman was in the car—Shelley Goldberg of NYI News. Well, we had a ball driving down.

I had no idea of what would the day would be. We arrived at Fort Dix, New Jersey, and parked in a lot and crawled on a bus to go to the range.

George had told us how to dress for the day, and we did. When we arrived, he introduced us to a number of FBI agents. We had coffee and then went outside to watch them do an enactment of a hostage situation. It was so realistic, and it was scary. I do not want to witness a real one.

We started over to the other side, and George informed us that we would do the shoot. I said, "George, I do not think I can do it."

He knew everyone there, and he had arranged for us to go first. They were handing us ear protection and eye goggles. *Oh my*, I thought. *So as not to embarrass George, I've got to do it.*

I made Shelley go first, and then I went. There were two hundred FBI agents watching, so I went with my Capricorn attitude. The instructor put the Glock in my hand with the safety on and showed me how to hold it straight out with both hands and find the middle of the target. He had his shoulder right up against mine. Now I know it was to keep me from pulling a Dick Cheney.

Well, I had my mark and fired away. Amazingly, I hit four out of six. It had a pretty good kick.

Then it was on to a machine gun like you see at

airports, Grand Central, or riding shotgun for the president. I got about three out of six. I was expecting a bigger kick on it, but there was not, which I found amazing.

The next one was another machine gun like the military uses, and I was acting like a pro with all the confidence in the world. I hit six out of ten. Wow.

I finished and walked off. Three or four young agents walked up and asked if I was an agent. "Oh, goodness, no; this is the first time I ever shot a gun," I replied.

They said, "You shoot better than we do." Of course, I am sure they were just kidding me.

Then I came face-to-face with a gentleman I recognized in the same gear as mine. He said, "You sound just like someone I know."

My face was pretty much covered, and I said, "What is her name?"

He said, "Nadine Schramm."

I laughed and said, "Sal, it is Nadine."

We had a good laugh, as he was my friend Dr. Sal Cumella, who introduced me to New York Women's Agenda. We were both out of our normal places, but wherever you went, Dr. Sal would be there.

What a day George Kalergios had given us. Of course, he loves to tell the story. He has given me many fun times with not just him but with his lovely family. He is the best person I have ever met to walk into a room with when you know no one. In ten minutes, you know most in the room.

If I have any regret in life, it is the relationship I have with my daughter, Mary. The trauma of her father's abuse has left a terrible toll on any stability in our relationship. He taught her that I had abandoned her, when in fact he disappeared with her, and I struggled for years before finding her. My friends and family all know the truth. She came to me after she grew up, and we had many good years, and she enjoyed a wonderful life with Bud and me. He was the father she never had with her blood father. Coming from the family life I had, it hurts terribly that I have been unable to share something similar with her.

Children are always the ones who suffer most. A child's mind is so easy to twist, and it is so sad that there are people who have no qualms about using children. I have gone way beyond with trying to make up for all. It's not enough.

She has always shared her children with me, and I have a great, loving time with them always. I'm so blessed that she gives me that. They are a very integral part of my life. They share their friends as well as their lives with me. When they were at the age of being so much fun to travel with and go out with my friends in the evenings, we did lots together. They have all finished college and are well on their way with good ethics and a feel for life that does not dwell much on the past. Always there are the things to deal with when parents divorce, but they handle it well. I am a very happy grandmother, and I revel in watching them grow into mature young people. I give a lot of credit to the parents. They raised three wonderful children.

I took a wonderful trip with interior decorator David Barrett and restaurateur John Miller on the great old sailing ship *Sea Cloud* that was built for Marjorie Merriweather Post of Post Cereals. We flew in to Sicily stayed overnight where twelve or so had a feast of seafood like I had never seen before. I did not know there were that many delicacies from the seas. It went on for hours with many bottles of wine.

The next morning, we got on board, and off we went to stop in many ports, ending in Venice. Well, John and David are both gay men who know how to dress and treat a woman like the queen bee. I had a ball. Every night, they invited me to their suite. We would have a drink, and then they would walk on either side of me for us to make a grand entrance down a long stairwell to the grand salon for the cocktail hour, which was always black tie.

There were lots more women than men, and about the third day, I went on deck to get sun, and four women from the Midwest were already there. I said hello, and we started to talk.

They said, "Nadine, you know, we kind of think it is unfair that you have two men when we are all single hoping to meet one."

David and John do not look gay, and I was not about to divulge it to this group that they were. I said, "We have been friends for a long time, and we planned to just get away by ourselves and catch up."

When I told them, they built it up more each day by showering me with attention. They are very creative, and one night after we got back from a day on shore, they decided to dress up like sheiks. They took sheets and white silk robes that they had brought with them and covered their heads. I went around and asked all the women on board if we could borrow their gold chains. That night, I walked in alone but with them just behind me. They pulled it off.

People assumed they must be very wealthy oilmen from the Middle East, and those four women were right there. There were not many passengers, so everyone got to know one another. I have wonderful pictures, and it was a most fun-filled trip.

John is tall, handsome, and always dressed in the best of everything. He and I went to lots of black tie affairs together. People would assume we were dating or married, and he loved playing with that. He said many times, "Oh, we have been together a long time but are not married." We both laughed a lot about it.

But now he has Jorge, so no more joking, and I am so happy for them. I gained a great hairdresser by meeting Jorge.

David Barrett has also passed away since I started this book.

John Miller took beautiful care of him in his last days—a true best friend.

I was having dinner in the main dining room of Smith & Wollensky one evening with the president and senior vice president of a bank who wanted my account and a mutual friend, Anthony Celano, co-owner of First Security, a security and investigative firm. One of the bankers had seats behind the plate at Yankee Stadium. It so happened that we were in a booth, and who was sitting behind me but Derek Jeter, the great baseball player—who had just retired this year—and his girlfriend.

The banker said that he would give anything to get Jeter's autograph. I called Tim, the manager, over and told him of the banker's wish, saying, "You know I would never ask for myself, but it would be a big favor for my friend."

Tim said, "I get five balls every year to have autographed. Let me see if I have one left."

Just a few minutes later, a ball was delivered to the

table next to us. I said, "Oh, my gosh, the waiter gave the ball to the wrong table. The woman at that table got up and went over to Jeter and got it signed and then left with her friends. Tim came over in a few minutes and asked if we got the autograph, and I told him what happened.

In the meantime, I had gotten up on my knees like a kid and asked Jeter if he would sign my friend's napkin for us, and he very generously did. I apologized for the interruption to his lady friend and said they should be asking for hers too. Such a total gentleman.

Tim asked, "You got the ball?"

I told him that the waiter had made a mistake. He went to the waiter, and it turned out that Tim had given the wrong booth number, and the woman knew she had gotten it by mistake.

They left, and there were two young men sitting in the middle of the dining room, and one started to choke. I said to my table of men, "That young man is choking. Do any of you know the Heimlich maneuver?"

None of them did, and I was amazed, but I pushed myself past them and called out to waiters, but no one made a move.

I grabbed the young man under the ribs and yanked. He was really heavy, but it was no problem because my adrenaline was in high gear. I lifted him two or three times before a piece of steak came up.

I sat back down, and several people came over and I asked me if I was a doctor or nurse. Of course, I said no. The young man came to the table and thanked me. I told him that he was one lucky man that I was there but that he'd better start chewing his food, because next time, I would not be there for him.

He said, "That's what my mother says."

I asked how much he weighed, and he said he weighed 270 pounds. It shows what you can do when you need to do. I had no pain from that lift the next day. It was my fourth save of chokers.

What a night we had. I hope I don't encounter any more chokers; I don't know if I could lift that much anymore. It's funny that three out of the four people I have saved from choking have been men. Okay, guys, chew your food.

There was another episode that several of us have laughed over a few times. It was with a group of us who would go to a restaurant called Campagnola on Thursday nights. We would have dinner by about 9:00 p.m. and then all go to Elaine's until the late hours.

One night, Adrienne Sutton and I left the restaurant

after our dinner, and as we walked out front, a car alarm went off. I thought it was funny. I went over and banged on the trunk, and it popped open. I flopped my butt in with feet straight up in the air. A bunch of young guys who knew us were out front, and they were laughing hard. I jumped out and slammed the trunk shut. The alarm stopped, and we were on our way.

There were lots of file folders, and we laughed that it was probably a lawyer or accountant. Maybe even a cheater?

We stayed at Elaine's until closing, and I started to pay the bill. I didn't have my glasses. I just thought I'd left them at the Campagnola. I called the next morning, but they did not have them. It dawned on me that my purse was not closed, and the glasses had fallen into the trunk. Oh boy, some man was in trouble if his wife found the pair of women's glasses—maybe even worse if he found them and wondered what he had done the night before. Well, that was an expensive laugh on me; it cost me $1,000 for those glasses. I bought a much cheaper pair the next time.

Adrienne got a call the next morning from one of the guys. He said the movie cameras should have been there. It was one of the funniest sights they had ever seen and should be a scene in a movie.

CHAPTER 16

The Work Ethic I Learned as a Farm Girl Pays off in the Big Apple

Bud was and I am a very strong supporter of Theatrical Teamsters Local 817. I sit on the board of the pension, welfare, and scholarship fund as Bud did. I use only theatrical drivers for my company, and they are the best. They know their business, and I respect them for their expertise. They are totally professional.

Tom had asked me to serve six months after Bud died. Local 817 is the only union in the country that sends members' children to college, paying for their education as well as board to any college of their choice if accepted. They must retain a certain grade level. Six hundred students have received degrees, many from top colleges.

I am fortunate to be treated very well by Theatrical Teamsters Local 817—expecting no special treatment and getting none. They have never questioned my ability in running a company very foreign to women. This is a business where there is no room for excuses. Any job we are on means many men are all working together, and if one person slacks off, then the others are slowed down. That cost business a lot of money. You won't last long if you do not go by the rules.

Walton Hauling and Budd Enterprises Ltd. are acutely aware of the needs; each is a family-owned business that has been in trucking over one hundred years and is not about to ruin family records.

There are many others in our business who feel the same. New York is totally geared to television, radio, theater, movies, and all elements of them.

I had begun to buy more trucks, as the need was there. Someone needed to step up to fill the need, so I did. I was buying two or three at a time.

I started a new corporation in the early 1990s when I started renting equipment to production companies, and I named it Budd Leasing Ltd. That kept the income separate from the work I did with labor charges. I also needed more mechanics. We now have three full-time mechanics and one part-time mechanic to make sure the trucks are in good running condition.

I have grown from the seven to eighty-two trucks. I am very comfortable in the role I play, but it would never have happened if the teamsters and customers did not accept a woman without prejudice. I never play the game of expecting any special treatment. From early childhood, boys and girls were equal in my family.

I love the way all the teamsters stick together and help each other out. They do not complain unless they have a real beef, and they should point out any infraction, as it is proper to do so.

People complain when filming is done in their neighborhood. There are disruptions, but many jobs are created. Local businesses are used by the crews for food, hardware, lumber, and so on. Local, state, and federal taxes paid are huge. It is very good for the economy of New York City and the state, being one of the largest for tax revenue.

Owning trucks, you know at sometime you will have accidents, but I have been very lucky, which I attribute to having very good drivers with the Theatrical Teamsters Local 817.

So I will tell you of a couple that I could laugh about, as they were so unusual.

I had a driver who evidently did not understand bridges in Central Park. He drove a truck, though I don't know how anyone could not notice that the bridge is very low and impossible to drive a truck under. Most drivers know not to go through the park.

I got the call from the driver that he had sheared off

the whole top of the truck and was now stuck under the bridge. A tow truck had to be called to pull him backward to Fifth Avenue. It was a big loss for me and no doubt the loss of a job with the union for him.

There was another situation that was not our driver's fault. He had a breakdown on the Long Island Expressway. He had markers out, and we had called a tow truck that was getting close to him. Thank God the driver had gotten out of the truck and was in front of it and not behind, because a tractor-trailer rig swerved off the highway and hit the back of the truck. The driver got out and said, "I can't believe I hit you." There was lots of damage to the truck, and my driver would have probably been dead if he had been behind it.

We sometimes get a few retired police officers and firemen who had retired young, and they make good drivers. Well, there was an exception on this one. A police officer who covered my neighborhood and who I knew had retired asked about working as a teamster. I was happy to recommend him, because I knew he was very reliable. He was put as a helper a few weeks later on a truck with a driver—a retired fireman on his first day as a teamster. They were in the Bronx, and the traffic was very heavy, so he angled off to go on a side road. The helper—so the story goes—said to him, "You need to stay on the main road, as there are probably overpasses on this route that will be too low."

He looked down, and the next thing he knew, they had hit an overpass, and it took the whole top of a truck off. It was lying behind the truck, and the driver panicked and wanted to leave the top.

The helper said, "No, we have to pick it up and put it in the truck. You need to call Nadine and tell her what happened." That was one call the poor guy did not want to make.

Reluctantly, he called. Well, needless to say, when the helper told me it was the guy's first day, I said, "Yes, first and last day as a teamster." And it was.

I love parties but had never celebrated my birthday, so I decided to give myself a large party. I knew others were planning to do a small dinner. I decided it was time in January 2010 and that I would make it very special. It was going to be the one and only, and I would spare nothing. I love giving parties and getting people together.

I asked one of my favorite Greek restaurants, Avra, if they would consider closing to the public on a Saturday night for me to take over for the evening.

They said yes and set a price to cover all expenses, including tips. I had it in my mind that it would be a party to be remembered, so it must be special in every way. I had so much fun planning, and I sent out save-the-date cards for January 16, though my birthday is on January 19. I wanted the party on a Saturday so that out-of-town guests would have time to travel and also to get over their hangovers.

The guest list was so important. I knew I could not have all I would love to have; that would have been just too many for any place to handle. I knew Avra could handle 180 and still have room for a musician and dance floor, which was a must for me.

I told Pam, my best friend, and she was going mad because she was afraid I would not do the party up right. I did everything myself, deciding the motif for save-the-date cards, the invitations, and the table decorations. I got many calls from people when they got the save-the-date cards, asking, "Are those your legs, feet, and shoes?" Yes, they were, and it's funny that lots of people knew they were mine. The card was a picture of my legs crossed at the feet with a pair of beautiful shoes. There was no doubt that it was my planning, as I love shoes, and I am loath to wear low heels unless it is for sports.

I love to dance. There is something about it that takes away any problem I have on my mind. I may not be the best dancer in the room, but no one has more fun doing a jig than I do. So I hired a piano player and singer who I had heard in Orlando when I was there at a convention. He played all the music I wanted for the party. It was good for dancing the night away, which we did. He took requests and everyone had a good time dancing and mixing. Now many bring it up as one of the best parties they ever went too. It was for me too; the only thing missing was Bud.

On the front of the invitation, I put a picture of a shoe with a fabulous bouquet of colorful flowers in it.

The message inside read:

> "Let's kick up our heels and celebrate life
> with cocktails, food, and dance."

> "Attire: festive, cocktail."

"Remember, you are only young once, but you can stay immature indefinitely. Take it from one who knows."

For the party, a shoe was on each table as the centerpiece with a colorful array of flowers.

I had twenty-six members of my family fly in from all over the country, and I made arrangements for them to make reservations in a hotel next door to me across the street from Avra.

I prepared food for all for two days just as they would do if I am in their home cities—lots of my favorite dishes. It was so much fun, and they did not have to go to restaurants for any food. It also gave us more time together.

Friends came from all over the country as well as

surrounding New York City. You name any profession, and it was represented; people were there from all walks of life. I would love to name all 180, as each and every one has added fond memories to my life. I will never be satisfied not making new friends and sharing their stories.

I have been to many parties, and I have never seen people mix, dance, and laugh as much as that party. I have chosen friends very carefully, and it showed. I love my friends.

People asked me if I was not worried having that many, and I said no. Actually, I was just going to a party; everyone was on their own. The food was fabulous, and the service was not to be compared at Avra. That night, I told all the service people, "As long as the food and drinks are served, you are to have a good time too." And they did.

I stood at the door as people came in. Each was photographed with me. The photographer was great, and she made sure each had a good picture to go in my album. I am so happy I did that, as I have a complete photo album of that night, and I pick it up often. Since the party, several are no longer with us, but I look at their pictures and smile. I know they had a great time that night.

I always say, "Smile; it costs nothing. Cry in happiness." It has been my motto for years, and for me it works. Try it; it might work for you too.

I was in Smith & Wollensky one night and standing at

the front of the bar talking and laughing with some regulars when Ollie, the bartender, said to me, "Nadine, there are some people in the back that are a group of umpires, and they want to know who the lady is that is laughing so much and having a good time. They would like you to join them."

Well, it was Linda Plunkett, who was the lady friend of Gerry Davis, the well-known baseball umpire who spent thirty years behind the plate. She was the only woman with a group of umpires. Of course, I went back and joined them.

This has turned into a wonderful friendship. They invited me to go to a Yankees game the next night. Gerry, of course, had to go very early afternoon. Then Linda said that she would pick me up. Well, here came a stretch limo. When we got to Yankee Stadium, we went down into the belly of it and got in the elevator, which was small. There was a young lady, and she said, "Nadine, what are you doing here? I met you last night downtown at the opening of a restaurant."

Then the man said, "I knew I had met you too; I was at the same party."

It was a small elevator, and two people called my name. I thought, *Boy, you'd better be careful what you say or do. It's a small world.*

We have become close friends, and they stay in my extra apartment when they come for games. We have so much fun; it's as if we've known each other forever. I was so happy that he gave her a ring at Christmas, and they planned to be married in November 2013. I felt so honored to be invited to the wedding.

Their relationship reminds me so much of the one I enjoyed with Bud. I know they will have a wonderful life together.

It seems in New York there is always a party being planned or happening, and some are very memorable.

In 2011 I got a call from Terry Lawler with New York Women in Film & Television, asking me to lunch. Of course, I went, and I felt very honored that she'd asked me.

At that luncheon, she asked me to be an honoree of the organization at their annual party. I am very happy to do anything to help people climb up that tall ladder, so of course I was very excited and agreed. It is a group I relate to, but I thought I would only know a few people. Well, of course, all my friends were there. This is a wonderful group of people who do so much to help women artists make it in a business that requires tenacity to succeed. They are an incredible support system.

I found out who else was being honored and realized that it was really going to test me. I had been to the luncheons before, but it's different when you are on stage. I really enjoyed it and met some lovely people that day. I was honored along with an impressive list of other women, including Claire Danes, Christine Baranski, Martha Stewart, and Marcie Bloom. I of course spoke a great deal about the same things I did at the NYWA breakfast.

Again, I had many who came up to thank me for talking about abuse. I got letters from some, and one touched me greatly. It was from a young woman from California, and she said she had been married for twenty years and abused all that time. She went home and filed for divorce. She wrote "You gave me the encouragement I needed."

One event of great significance was in March 2012 at the retirement party for Thomas O'Donnell, the president of Theatrical Teamsters Local 817. He was president for fifty-one years, and when I first met him back in the 1960s, the hall was on Ninth Avenue in a building that was old and not in a good neighborhood. In fact, it was less than safe at the time.

He started the pension, welfare, and scholarship fund in 1965. I still do not think any compare to it. He was a man whom everyone admired and who truly deserved it. He gave up much in his own life to see that the union grew at an astounding rate. He was a visionary who worked so hard to help others. He helped his men and also all the companies that had anything to do with television and movies or were in any way connected to the entertainment industry. He was honest to a fault, if that can be said of anyone. He demanded honesty and fair negotiations. I am proof that he did not discriminate against women. Back in those days, not many would have expected that a woman would run a trucking company for these supposedly tough men.

Never once have any of them treated me differently from the way they treated men in our industry, and I do not expect it to be different.

He asked me to join the board of the pension plan as an owner.

His son, Tom, and daughter, Christine, asked me help them find a venue for his retirement party, which was no small task, as the number of people to be invited was huge. I made many calls, and the biggest venue was the Sheraton on Seventh Avenue, and even it would not hold all that needed to be invited, but a line had to be drawn. There was lots of planning, and the union office did all the invitations and planning, which had to be very difficult.

It was a beautiful event, and I was very honored to be asked to speak that evening. It was a bittersweet time for me, as he was such a trusted friend whom I loved working with. I know no one else who affected so many lives.

Unfinished Business

It was hard to see him in a wheelchair. That very strong man now needed someone to help him. He was in a separate room for about two hours to greet a lot of people. I sat next to him, as he was having trouble remembering all of them. Well, there were many I did not know, but I covered for him by asking their names so he could pick up on them. (I should add here that I also have trouble remembering all the people who have been in my life. It comes with age.) Rarely a day goes by without thoughts of him and his wonderful wife, Phyllis.

He would never let anyone pick up a tab. One time only a few years before he died, we had all gone to a funeral upstate, and he and I decided to stop for lunch in a small place on the way back. I said, "Tom, I want to buy lunch today. No one knows us, so you have no excuse for me not buying."

He said, "No, *I* would know." He was one man you would never win an argument with, so he paid.

We have lost him, and if he had lived to one hundred years old, it would not have been enough.

Tommy, his son, is now the president, and he has all the experience he needs, as he has actually been the one who was there for a great number of years before Tom stepped down. He is very smart and no doubt will do many good things for the members.

The main reason for this book is to let every woman who is abused know from my own experience what they need to do. They must admit to themselves that if a man hits once, he will continue. No one can change him. The hardest part is admitting to others that you are being abused and hiding it. Ask for help. If you are afraid, go to the authorities; most police stations are now required to investigate any reports.

Abusers' greatest method of control is simply your shame of admitting what they are doing. To anyone who is abused, I say if I could be on a bandstand anywhere and preach, I would say no matter how hard, grab somebody by the hand and say, "Please help me. I am afraid for my life, but I do not know how to get away. But with help, I will."

I recently read in the newspaper that one-third of women report being abused by a husband or boyfriend at some point in their lives. I am not surprised.

You would be surprised how much help you will get if you ask. I did when I was to the point where I knew I was going to have a nervous breakdown or he would actually kill me. I had lost all hope. I had hit the bottom of my endurance, and I was no longer embarrassed to say, "I am captive of a man who gives me black eyes regularly, who mentally and physically abuses me every day." Many times, mental abuse is worse than physical, as bruises heal, but mental injuries last for a long time.

I would hate to be the person who ever lays a hand on me now. I would not kill, but I can assure you that person would probably wish to die.

There is still no help from some officials. Read the papers, and every day you see—even in New York with all our services—that there are many cases of abuse. Abuse of women is often ignored, and sometimes men will ask, "What did she do to provoke it?"

However, we do have agencies that of are of major help, and one of the most noted is the office of District Attorney Charles Hynes of Brooklyn. He has a master plan in place and is very successful in the handling of abuse. I have seen the facility, and it is secure from any harassment by the abuser. I was very impressed. You have to go through turnstiles after telling at a desk first where you are going and who you are seeing. If you do not have an appointment name, you will not get in. His program is readily available to any city or state that would like to start such a program.

I will personally take all the time anyone needs to help them get away from abuse. I have no training in this, but I have certainly had experience. I know that the abusing men are all so much alike; they are insecure, and they think it makes them look big if they can control a woman. They are like cookie-cutter cutouts.

I have had a wonderful life, and it is still very exciting to me.

I rarely ever think of my age, although the numbers are there.

My business is still growing. I now have eighty-two trucks and counting, including tractors and trailers. I started with seven straight. I could never have done all this without having wonderful people working for me and so many loyal customers.

Kelly has been hired by a major pharmaceutical company. Amanda finished college and went to nursing school and got her degree. She is now working in a hospital. Anyone will be lucky to get her in sickness. She was asked by mothers of newborn babies to sit when she was about six, so I was not surprised with her choice.

Darrell Tetreault, who worked in the office with me, is now married to my granddaughter Amanda. He decided he wanted to be a Connecticut state trooper. I hated to lose him, but he had my blessing to go with his dreams, and he is a commanding figure in that uniform.

After Darrell left, Ryan O'Toole, who went to college with my grandson, Michael, was looking for a job just at the right time for me. He has been a godsend to me, as he has learned every aspect of trucks as well as all the details in the business. The teamsters all enjoy working with him.

This is an office where you get answers, and if you are promised a call back, you will get it from us. We are very organized with every aspect of the business. When you call us, we are going to fill the needs, and always with laughter. We have gotten to the point that we know many of the teamster captains well and have a great rapport with them. There are never excuses; we just get things done. It is the easy way.

When problems arise, we follow through and make sure they are resolved quickly and effectively. All of us are on call 24-7. If a teamster needs something at 5:00 a.m. or 10:00 p.m., we are there to help. Our customers know that they can always depend on us.

We were damaged heavily during Hurricane Sandy. There was no place to take so many trucks, so we had to stay put except for tractors, which I had moved to higher ground because they were close to the water. The storm hit with a vengeance. I could not believe how high the water came up even though we were on the water's edge of the East River in Greenpoint, Brooklyn, that sits up high. I immediately called a truck-washing company and had them come and wash off under the trucks to get off all the salt water. It was very important to get them washed immediately, as salt works very fast on metal. We still had major damage. I made the call to repair, because the industry would have been in real trouble not having trucks for all the filming being done.

There was not a question in my mind about repairing or declaring the trucks a total loss. We had to choose to repair in order to keep the business. It would have been the end of filming in New York if suppliers did not get back up and running. The insurance company sent an adjuster from Saint Louis, Missouri, to work with us for days so that we could continue to service all. The easy way would have been to cash out, but I could not do that; there were too many jobs at stake. And now we are back to normal.

I hope this book gives men and women the encouragement in life to do anything they wish. Believe in yourself. Do not be afraid to try anything. Remember there was that day when you were a child and you had to take that very first step. Life is just another step every day.

In closing, *can't* should not be in your vocabulary. It is self-defeating.

If there are men reading this book who are abusers, see a therapist. You are also putting yourself in the position of actually killing someone.

I hope you have received the needed encouragement to better your life by reading this book.

I do put in more hours at work than many people, but it always is because I have never had a business that I did not love. When I get up in the morning, I am already wondering what fun I am going to have instead of "Oh my, what next will ruin my day?" I do not entertain negative thoughts. If you think you are going to have a bad day, it is almost guaranteed you will. I do have some that are not perfect, but I do not dwell on them, and I try to work out any problems with a positive attitude.

Sometimes I think I laugh and smile more in a week than many do in a lifetime. I always say to anyone who is unhappy with their work, "Go to what you really love, as you will never be successful in a dull and unpleasant job where you do not get up excited every day." There are about a million things you can pick from unless you happen to live in an area where there are only a few jobs. If possible, make the move where you have more choices.

My telephone is always answered on a happy note even when it is 5:00 a.m. and a teamster needs another truck or perhaps has a problem with one. There are never any excuses; we just take care of it. It is so much easier on your system, including your heart, stomach, and laugh lines. Do you ever really enjoy being around someone who is always complaining? Most of those people spend a lot of time alone. Wonder why?

CHAPTER 17
One Happy Family

Here, I will introduce all my brothers and sisters who have been such an important factor in my life.

The oldest is Inez, who married a New Yorker. The marriage ended in divorce, but she stayed in New York until she retired. She worked at Manny Wolf's, a restaurant that became Smith & Wollensky. When it sold, she went to one of their others the Old Homestead Steakhouse, which is still there. Greg and Mark Sherry, who were just children when Inez worked for their parents at Manny Wolf's, still talk to me about her. They loved her—and with reason. She handled all the cash long before credit cards, and they knew they could trust her. She retired back to Arkansas but ended up running a women's organization's luncheons.

Gladys married a career navy man, Pete Henningson, from Saint Louis, Missouri, who had been adopted by an elderly aunt and uncle. He had gone in the service at seventeen, signing his own papers instead of the aunt or uncle who were supposed to sign. He was in Hawaii when Pearl Harbor was bombed. He had shore leave that Saturday night. He got drunk in a bar and went home with a young lady. When he heard the bombing in the harbor early Sunday morning, he ran to get back to his ship. He saw the devastation with his ship being one hit, and all his friends were gone. He always said that young lady saved his life, and he did not even know her name.

A few years later, he was sent to Fort Smith as a navy recruiter. When he married Gladys, he was in heaven with a large new family, and he made it well known to all how lucky he was. We were blessed; he was a beautiful human being who gave so much to all of us and especially to our sister, who had one of the worst cases of eye problems very early in life.

I was in high school, and he was my biggest rooter at basketball games. He died of cancer much too young. He smoked too many cigarettes, as much of our population still do. I went back only a few weeks before he died at the age of fifty-seven to help out all the family with caring for him. He was so worried because I was coming, and he could see the car was dirty. He made sure it was clean before I got there to drive it. He always worried about others even when he was in such terrible pain.

My poor sister lost someone she dearly loved and

someone who had become her eyes. He spoiled her; anything she wanted was hers. After he had retired, they spent a lot of time going to yard sales and auctions. When I went to visit before he was sick, we went all over having so much fun. They ended up with a huge collection of china and glassware. Gladys never complained, but she had lost the man who was her guardian angel. They had two children, Marvin (Butch) and Maren, a daughter. Butch became a teacher out of the University of Arkansas, and Maren went into nursing and is now is a hospice nurse. Maren was only sixteen when her father died.

Gladys stayed in her own home with help and then in a nursing home. She just recently passed at the age of eighty-nine.

Frances married Steve Teufel from Milwaukee, Wisconsin. He went overseas just after they were married. Frances came home to live with us—pregnant with her oldest son, Shelby, who carries our family name—until he got back home.

One time—and though I laughed when I was a youngster, it scares me today—she was in the yard, and a washtub was there. She bent over to pick something up and lost her balance and fell with her stomach in the tub and could not get out of it. She was probably eight months pregnant and big. I started laughing and then realized the major problem, and I could not lift her. I ran in to get my mother. We worried that perhaps the baby had been hurt, but thank God she was okay, and Shelby was born a very healthy boy.

They had three children—Shelby, Barbara, and Larry. Larry has the family ailment of retinitis pigmentosa.

Ralph married Nita Floren from Muskogee, Oklahoma. She had one brother and a mother and father who were much older, so she was not used to our big family. She had to listen to many stories of ours, especially the girls when we all got together. I apologized years later for how rude we were, and she said, "Well, it's okay because now I have many stories to add."

They also had three children—Eugene, JoAnne, and Christina (Tina). Eugene is a doctor in Hot Springs, Arkansas; JoAnne has been active working for politicians in Little Rock, Arkansas; and Tina has lived and worked in Little Rock and Hot Springs. Tina started her own business when she graduated from the University of Arkansas, where she studied horticulture.

Ralph and Nita also had a daughter who died as a baby of stomach cancer.

Annette married Carroll Moore in the army from Greenwood, South Carolina. He was another great guy who took on a big responsibility in helping with the genetic eye problem, and there was never a "poor me" act.

Annette worked at Arkansas Best Freight in Fort Smith when she graduated. Her picture still hangs in their offices. In Greenwood, South Carolina, she worked at Belk's department store for all the rest of her working years, and she worked until she was in her sixties. She counted all the money long before credit cards. Her eyesight was bad from a very young age, and she did not have good health. As a youngster and not understanding her health issues, I just thought she did not want to work in the fields. She was smart, always earning straight *A*'s, and she was valedictorian of her class.

She continued to work at Belk, and when her eyesight grew worse, her husband would drive her and then walk her to the door, where she would be met by the manager, who then took her through the store and upstairs to her office. When her sight got to the point where she could no longer read the print, they ordered a large sheet of magnifying glass to put over her machines so she could continue. She was now handling all the sales receipts from all their stores plus payroll. They never wanted her to retire, but she finally did.

She had a woman named Roberta who did all her housework, and when Carroll passed away, Roberta took over all the household chores and drove Annette where she needed to be.

I lost her just as I was finishing up this book. They had one child, Cheryl, who has the eye problem. Cheryl has no siblings to depend on. She was married but later divorced, and she lives in South Carolina, where none of our family members are. Her father's family lives there, and they are very helpful, and Roberta remains there when she can.

Jim married a woman from Kentucky. He was too good many times, and when he owned a gas station, he would give anyone free gas who came by with a bunch of kids or a good sob story. Needless to say, he went broke. He was the only one in our family who got into trouble. He could not drink even a small amount of liquor, but it took him a long time and many bar room fights before he gave it up. He was short in stature but built like a bull, and some friends would tell me he would take on a full barroom.

Our poor father bailed him out from jail many times. I begged him to stop getting him out. My father said to me, "He's my son; he is still my responsibility." I never again questioned him. Jim did give up drinking when he married.

All of my family loved company. The girls all know how to cook for crowds, because we learned from our mother. I kind of missed out on the kitchen work since I always worked in the fields. Today I am the one who cooks for friends with great gusto, and they are always asking when I am having another dinner party.

Unfinished Business

For many years after he married, everything seemed good with Jim and his wife, Carol, but then it became very nasty when he had lost all his sight. She became a very mean person and would not let any family members in to see him. He was totally blind. She wanted the three sisters who lived in Fort Smith to take care of him, but two were already legally blind, and Inez was working ten to twelve hours a day running a women's club. I was already married to Bud, and I went back there for a visit. I was mad as hell. She was keeping him locked in the house, and while she was at work, they would talk to him through the window in his bedroom, afraid to open the door.

Well, my niece Nancy and I went over, and I told him it was me, and I said, "Jim, I am not leaving till you open the door."

He said, "I can't; she has given me orders not to let any member of the family in."

I said, "I am your sister. This is not right, and I am not leaving town till I see you."

I heard him fumbling but going to the door in the back of the house. She had the door barricaded from the inside, and he was moving things aside.

We finally got in. He looked terrible and said he had been very sick. He had been so handsome. He was very nervous. He asked if we would like a Coke, and we said yes. He said, "Be sure to take the bottles with you when you go, or she will know someone has been here."

We told him how all were calling her wanting to see him, and we told him how we all loved him. He said, "I have no choice but to do as she says, but I miss my family."

We purposely stayed, and sure enough, she came home. We were sitting in the living room, and she burst in and said to me, "You know you are not supposed to be here."

I said, "He is my brother, and you are holding him hostage, and I will not leave."

I told her that either she had to let me in or I would go to the authorities. She said, "I am leaving, but when I get back, you two had better be gone."

I felt such pain, but I had no choice. We hugged and kissed him, and as we left, I knew I would never see him again. He died shortly after.

I had come back to New York. Jim's wife had him cremated and then called one of the sisters to say he was dead and cremated. It was not what he would have wanted; he had seen our house burn, and I knew he was as afraid of fire as I was. He died alone and then was treated like garbage. She left very shortly with an older man. She now lives in Florida. A brother-in-law tracked her recently. He found that our brother's ashes were buried in Fort Smith National Cemetery—not where our parents are, as well as the twin Mary Lou, Inez, and then our youngest brother, Harry.

At least we are now at peace knowing where he is. Was it not easy for her to tell us instead of finding him almost twenty years later—and only after our brother-in-law David Byrd searched records until he traced it all?

Martha Sue, the twin, married Henry "Hank" Graney from Saint Charles, Illinois, who was is the service in Fort Chaffee, Arkansas. He had been married before, and when Hank asked for Martha's hand, Daddy sat them down and talked to them. Hank had two children from a previous marriage, and Daddy said, "You must take care of your two children from your first marriage before you have any children together and before Martha gets anything. If you are willing to do this, you have my blessing." And they did.

They went on to have five of their own, but they also took care of his first two. We lost Martha Sue much too soon. She did not draw good cards healthwise. She had the eye problem and then had a double mastectomy by the time she was forty. She had surgery for breast implants, but it did not work. She cried because she thought that it was unfair for Hank to have a wife with a scarred body and no bust. Bless Hank—he told her, "I did not marry you for your body; I married you because of who you are as a human being, and that has not changed."

Well, they had great love, and then she had a double aneurysm. Hank was home at the time. She was on the phone with our brother Ralph, and she just dropped it and collapsed. Hank called 911 for the local volunteer ambulance group.

They lived in a beautiful big old farmhouse outside Chicago, which they needed with such a large family. It was lucky that the ambulance was just three hundred feet from the entrance to their home when he called. If not, she would not have survived.

The three days of agony waiting until they could operate was nerve-racking. We were all on the phone constantly with each other and praying more than for anything before. She survived, but it was a very long and tough way back with learning to speak and growing her hair again. She never complained, and then, not many years later, the cancer came back, and that time, nothing would help.

They raised beautiful children, but it was so hard on them. They all pulled together and insisted on keeping her home. Some of us made trips to stay a week or so. She died in 1997 with all of them taking turns holding her. I have never seen such love. The young children had seen their mother suffer so much, and yet they did all the things necessary and everything to make her comfortable. She died with all of them there holding her. They have all turned out to be such a close, loving family. She never ever asked, "Why me?" It has been the same with all our family with tragedy. To the very end, she seemed so at peace.

When I look back, she must have been so tired. She had lost her twin at six months and always said she felt half of her was missing. I do not shed tears often, but I still tear up writing this. She had such faith and strength. Hank has never remarried, and I understand why. What a beautiful love affair.

Neta, the youngest girl, married a local, David Byrd. They have had their share of taking care of family members. They should have a special place in heaven. They still live in Fort Smith. They make all the hospital and nursing home visits and are there when family members pass away.

Neta also has the eye problem. It does not slow her down much; she still whizzes around her own kitchen. They have three children, two boys and a girl. The two boys are nearly blind because of that debilitating eye problem. They never complain; what strong people.

Neta and David have a great sense of humor and are always telling jokes or talking about pranks they have pulled. Bud and I had been to New Orleans, and in a club, they were selling a can similar to the big tin used for fruit drinks that had a label that said Southern Poontang, so of course Bud bought a couple of them to bring back to

New York. We kept one, and he wrapped the other and mailed it to David.

A couple of weeks later, David sent an enveloped edged in red with note inside that read, "Where can I get a refill?" Now to all you men who do not know about poontang, do not throw the word around until you know what is. You could ask any Southern man, but I will tell you that it means sex in a can.

Neta and David had three children. Sheila, who is a first-grade teacher, put in a program that is heavily used in Arkansas schools. She had each child put a few dollars into an account at the local bank. She then took them to meet the bank manager. They then bought material and made little items for sale. In other words, she taught them how to make a business plan. Then they sold the items and put the money in the bank. She has done this for over twenty-five years. Everyone in the school system talks about her and about what she has taught them about saving money. She now has children of the ones she taught twenty-five years ago. She has just been awarded a national award to be given to her in Baltimore, Maryland. She has received several from the State of Arkansas.

David Martin, their oldest son, went to the University of Arkansas, and his thesis was written on Walmart. He always knew he wanted to work there, and he got an interview.

The man interviewing him could not believe David Martin knew all their financials and finally excused himself and went in to Sam Walton and told him about David. Sam Walton said he would like to meet that young man. David could not believe he was actually going to meet Mr. Walton.

The way he told it was that when he went in, Sam Walton said, "I understand you know my figures as well as I do, if not better. Sit down; I want to talk to you." He kept him for an hour and then called the interviewer in and said, "Hire this young man."

The man asked, "And where would you like me to put him?"

Sam said, "Anywhere he wants."

He put David in a small store in Arkansas as assistant manager when he was only twenty-two years old. He went on to open many stores, and when they started opening the big megastores, he was put in charge of stocking several of them for grand openings.

He has the eye disease and finally had to retire at a young age. Well, he has a hobby, much to everyone's good fortune who has been able to share it with him: he is a barbecue king. He has a way that's his own and his own recipe. His takes it to nursing homes and other places to share. He also has a dog that he has trained to go to the nursing homes and hospitals.

Then Brent, the youngest, also had the eye problem at a younger age than most, and he had to retire from Walmart. He has the best group of male friends who take him everywhere. He is a great sports fan and has a room decorated with sports, and they all spend a lot of time there for games.

Dink—which is Neta's nickname for him—and David are the ones who now carry the burden of being the ones left for all of us when we get together in Fort Smith.

She cooks for days, and she would put many chefs to shame. There is only one problem with being in her home: I always come back weighing two or three pounds more than before I went there.

We do have nieces there, and they do their share of entertaining too.

Harry, the youngest brother, never married. He stayed home with our parents until both passed, and then he bought his own home. He retired from Whirlpool, where he worked his whole life. He bought a dirt bike to ride with his buddies in the country. He loved it and enjoyed being retired.

In May 2006, he bought a new bike and took on what was to be a five-minute test drive. He went on a state highway just up from his house. He was not five minutes into Charleston when a fellow he had known all his life pulled out from a side road and hit him broadside. The man should not have been driving because his eyesight so bad, as we found out later. Harry was taken to a hospital in Fort Smith, where he endured seventeen hours of surgery by three different groups of surgeons. He lived, but they were not good years; virtually everything had been damaged in the accident. The doctors said that the odds of him even surviving the crash were almost nil, and then he had to have all the surgeries. He had a will to live, with dialysis twice a week and all the other things.

He made many trips from the assisted-living facility to the hospital. Neta and David were on call most of the time. We lost our baby brother three years later. The doctors said he was tougher than Evel Knievel ever was.

He wanted to live badly. Anyone else I think would have given up much sooner. The Shelby family is a tough bunch. He died January 31, 2009, from the injuries caused by the accident.

We all need to get our priorities in order. Life can give you new ones quickly.

Watch all my family with retinitis pigmentosa, and you see true love. First of all, none of them sit and do nothing, but they do require an arm to hold on to when outside the home. I think this may cause a more intimate relationship. How many couples do you know who hold hands a lot?

All of them are excellent cooks; just stay out of their kitchen, and don't move things around. They know each item, and it always goes back where it came from. Otherwise, they would have to ask someone to find it for them.

We have a family reunion every year. When our parents were alive, the reunions were always in Arkansas, but now we go different places, and everyone goes unless there is some real problem with scheduling.

I miss the reunions more than most. They are almost always in June or July, because that's when the children are not in school. It is my time for Concerts in the Park for the Metropolitan Opera and the New York Philharmonic. However, I have gone to many of them.

I never go a day without thinking how lucky I have been. I have had no problem with eyes, no health issues at my age, and do not have to take any pills. I have energy that very young people do not have—or is it that they simply do not use theirs? I never waste an hour or a day. I am beyond blessed.

I have had three doctors in my life who are my general practitioners. I interviewed each to see if they were pill pushers. I always told them I wanted to interview. They all said okay. As I sat in one waiting room, I noticed about a dozen patients coming out with prescriptions in hand. I walked in and told him, "I noticed each patient came out with a prescription. That's the reason I wanted to talk to you before using you. I am not a pill taker except when absolutely needed."

He said, "Well, that's what people always want, so I fill their needs." I got up, thanked him, and walked out.

Then I found exactly the one for me. However, a few months later, I developed a slight problem with my stomach. I went in and told him my problem. He said, "Well, you are going to laugh when I tell you what to do. Go buy this book for $3.99 and choose what you want to do."

I did, and I ate more bran. End of problem. I have had a few minor things, but nothing major. I knew I had found the doctor for me.

Do I take it for granted to have good health? No, never. I still go to that office after forty-five years.

Dr. John Rodman is now the only one left at that office on East Fifty-Seventh Street, and he has been my doctor for many years.

I have been so fortunate with my health, and each year, I have my physical. If he feels I need to be checked for something he does not cover, he sends me to others.

I know how lucky I am. I try to eat healthily, and I do get exercise. I walk most everywhere I go—yes, always in high heels. Heels are simply the most comfortable for me;

after all these years, my body is simply used to them. I walk not to save money but because I love to. I have never gone to a gym even though I belong to the New York Athletic Club. I only go there to eat.

Dancing is my best exercise. I have no problem turning on music and dancing my heart out alone. I happen to like all the things that are good for me. We grew up with fresh fruit and vegetables on the farm. Then for meat it was chicken more than beef, as the beef was sold or used for milking.

I feel very strongly about the use of medication in this country. It seems that people pop pills for every minor thing. I think more damage is done many times than going without. The body does heal many things on its own. It was made to do so except when a major imbalance occurs. I have been so fortunate at my age to have never needed medication and to have never had any serious illness.

I did get a few calls from Tom Alten after I married Bud. One of his messages to me at 2:00 a.m. was "So you think you are so smart? I will ruin your marriage."

I raised my voice—something I have done maybe five times in my life. I told him that night, "Call me one more time, and I will kill you. I no longer care, and you have done so much damage to me and Mary that I will even things in one minute. I am no longer afraid of you, but you should be afraid of me." I never got another call. I wish I had done it sooner, but better late than never.

Tom Alten ended a miserable life with very poor health. I prayed that he would live a very long life in misery, and he did. His sister took him in during his long sickness.

I will never forgive him. He did too much damage to my daughter and me. The teachings of forgiveness do not work for me when so much evil is involved. I do not think I will go to hell for it. I was already there. And my daughter has scars never to heal.

Writing about my life with Tom has been very strenuous for me. I am again living the horror in my mind while writing some of it. If it convinces one woman to have the courage to run from abuse, it will be well worth it.

I ask any woman out there in trouble to look at what my life turned out to be. That is the purpose of writing the book. I hope thousands do the same as I did—just much faster. It is still no piece of cake, but ask for help.

I many times still think of how maybe I could have changed things so that Mary did not suffer as she has. It is very painful to live with that. But I know in my heart I did the best I could with the knowledge I had and the fact that there was little help available.

Look at how much happiness I had with Bud. You maybe will find your Bud. I have to admit that I always said that we had been so lucky to be so happy. Most people never have the happiness and love we did for twenty-six years. How could I complain? We were a totally perfect match.

I also said that God must have looked down on me after the first one and said, "Oh, I really messed up with her. Let me now give her the best." And he did.

Something happened recently, and I can now laugh about it. I went to a well-known psychic reader, Jeffery Wands, and all of a sudden in my reading, he said, "There is someone coming in, and he is asking for your forgiveness of his being so mean to you during your marriage to him."

Without a second's hesitation, I said, "Tell him to get back into hell."

Jeffery laughed.

I can now laugh about it, too.

Printed in the United States
By Bookmasters